Copyright © 1997 MGR Publishing & Promotions Inc.
Toronto, Canada

Photography: Clive Champion, Chris Freeland, Robert Wigington
Food Stylists: Joan Ttooulias, Dennis Wood, Clare Stancer
Prop Stylist: Karen Martin
Recipe Editor: Mary Merlihan
French Version: Louise Boyer, Jocelyne Gingras
Cover/Inside Design & Art Direction:
Dave Hader/Studio Conceptions

Pictured on front cover:
Sparkling Fruits in Strawberry-Kiwi Jelly

**KRAFT, JELL-O, JELS, JIGGLERS, SNACKTIVITIES, STILL THE
COOLEST, COOL WHIP, PHILADELPHIA, BAKER'S and KOOL-AID
are registered Trade Marks of Kraft Canada Inc.**

Acknowledgements:

Among the many people who helped to produce this book, we would like
to especially acknowledge Cécile Girard-Hicks, Director of the JELL-O
Kitchens and her enthusiastic staff of food professionals including:
Barb Martyn, Michele McAdoo, Maxine Karpel, Susanne Stark, Marian
Macdonald, Marilynn Small, Judy Welden and Jane Carman.

Questions? Call the JELL-O Hotline. Your call will be answered by an
experienced food professional—one of the helpful staff in the JELL-O
Kitchens.

The JELL-O Hotline is open Monday to Friday 9:00 a.m. until 4:00 p.m.
(E.S.T.). Any questions or comments, please feel free to call
1-800-268-7808.

Canadian Cataloguing in Publication Data

Main entry under title:
The Magic of JELL-O

Canadian ed.
Issued also in French under title: **La magie de JELL-O**
Includes index.
ISBN 0-9681850-0-2

1. Cookery (Gelatin).   2. Desserts.

TX814.5.G4M32 1997   641.8'64   C97-900203-6

Printed in Canada

The Magic of JELL-O*

DESSERTS & SNACKS

100 New and Favourite Recipes
Celebrating 100 Years of Fun with JELL-O

▼ ▼ ▼

MGR Publishing & Promotions Inc.

Toronto, Canada

A great team has worked very hard to put this book together for you. From left to right: Susanne Stark, Cécile Girard-Hicks, Michele McAdoo, Barb Martyn.

Dear JELL-O Consumer,

We invite you to celebrate this historical JELL-O moment with us.

JELL-O is now 100 years old - we like to think of it as 100 years young — so we've gathered 100 of the top-rated JELL-O ideas of all time and put them in this memorial cookbook to you.

We can't think of another food that has been so popular for so many years - to so many people of all ages. Nothing feels like JELL-O in your mouth, dances like JELL-O on your plate. Nothing can go from simple to sophisticated so easily.

This cookbook will take you from the JELL-O classics you enjoyed growing up to the latest up-to-the-minute products and recipes. Everything from our ready-to-eat line of jelly and pudding snacks to simple, sensational recipes for things like Trifle and Cappuccino Cups.

There's a section for novices and experts alike; a special section for kids; another one for the health-conscious called Light Delights. (It's reassuring to know that JELL-O Jelly Powder is fat free and very low in calories.)

Everything in this book has been tested in our own kitchens to make sure it's as easy as it can be and because we know how much you like to see what you're making, we have a photograph with each recipe.

The magic of JELL-O is all here for you to rediscover and we hope you have as much pleasure making these recipes as we did putting them together.

From the food experts of the JELL-O Kitchens

▼▼▼▼▼▼
CONTENTS

▼▼▼

JELL-O Brand
100 years and Still the Coolest!

For 100 years **JELL-O** Brand Jelly Powder has wiggled and jiggled its way into Canadian meals and celebrations. Today, if placed end to end, the 299 million packages of **JELL-O** Jelly Powder produced each year in North America, would stretch three-fifths of the way around the globe. More than 150,000 packages of **JELL-O** Jelly Powder are purchased in Canada every day. The **JELL-O** brand also offers calorie-reduced light flavours, instant and cooked puddings, and ready-to-eat gelatin and pudding snack cups.

The **JELL-O** story began more than 150 years ago. In 1845, Peter Cooper, an American industrialist, inventor and philanthropist obtained the first patent for a gelatin dessert. Although Cooper packaged his gelatin in neat little boxes with directions for use, he did very little with it. Home cooks still relied on sheets of prepared gelatin, which had to be clarified by boiling with egg whites and shells and dripped through a jelly bag before they could be turned into shimmering moulds.

An Inauspicious Beginning

Fifty-two years after Cooper obtained his patent, in 1897, Pearl B. Wait a carpenter and cough medicine manufacturer from LeRoy, New York, decided to enter the packaged food business. Looking for a product, he came up with a fruit-flavoured version of Cooper's gelatin. Since products ending in "O" were popular at the time, the product was christened "**JELL-O**" by his wife, May Davis Wait, and was available in strawberry, raspberry, orange and lemon flavours. For nearly two years Pearl Wait tried to sell the **JELL-O** product door-to-door, but he lacked the capital and sales experience to

Canada's Most Famous Dessert

READY IN MINUTES

market it properly. In frustration, Wait sold the **JELL-O** business in 1899 for $450 to his LeRoy neighbour, Orator Francis Woodward, an entrepreneur who founded the Genesee Pure Food Company a few years earlier and had successfully marketed "Grain-O", a roasted cereal beverage. Woodward's first year sales were so poor that one day, after touring the plant and seeing **JELL-O** cases piled high, he offered the business to his plant superintendent for $35, a new low for the fledgling product. The offer was refused. With the turn of the century came a new lease on life for the **JELL-O** brand. Helped along by Woodward's creative sales and sampling strategies, the product began to catch on and soon after the Canadian **JELL-O** tradition began.

The JELL-O Girl

The brand's first trademark, the **JELL-O** Girl, made her debut in 1903, as the star of Woodward's second advertising campaign. Elizabeth King, the daughter of Franklin King, an artist for the Genesee Pure Food Company's advertising agency, was shown playing in her nursery with **JELL-O** packages. The **JELL-O** Girl became the cornerstone of the **JELL-O** ad campaign for several years in Canada and was often seen with the slogan "**JELL-O**—Canada's Most Famous Dessert," or "Poudre **JELL-O**—le plus Fameux Dessert du Canada".

JELL-O's First Canadian Plant Debuts in Bridgeburg, Ontario

By 1906, Canadian **JELL-O** sales were on the rise, so the Genesee Pure Food Company built a factory in Bridgeburg, Ontario, which is now a part of

▼ ▼ ▼ ▼ ▼ ▼

Fort Erie, to handle the Canadian production. The new plant was quite modern and a series of advertisements issued invitations to the public, "We are really proud of the beautiful **JELL-O** kitchens at Bridgeburg, Ontario. If ever you are near Bridgeburg, come and see **JELL-O** made. You will be very welcome."

Kewpies* Sell the Jell-O Brand

In 1908, artist Rose O'Neill, who created the famous cheerful Kewpie Dolls, modernized the look of the **JELL-O** product with one of her renderings finding its way into the package design. Several of Canada's Kewpie ads promoted the **JELL-O** brand as the perfect "fun" dessert for children — easy to make, sweet and delicious. During this time, ads also portrayed **JELL-O** Jelly Powder as a good food for sick children or adults. **JELL-O** Jelly Powder was approved by food commissioners and praised as a pure, wholesome and appetizing food, endorsed by physicians and sugar-free jelly powder was prescribed for diabetic diets.

Canada's First JELL-O Recipe Book

In 1911, the first Canadian recipe book was created. It emphasized ease of preparation, low cost, purity, perfection and the variety of flavours that could be used to create delicious desserts. **JELL-O** packaging was updated in 1914 with automatic equipment and a new seamless sealed wax paper bag, which was more effective in keeping moisture out.

The 1920s Bring Major Changes

In 1923, the Genesee Pure Food Company changed its name to the **JELL-O** Company of Canada, in a move to protect its famous trademark. In another bold corporate move, Canadian **JELL-O** production was moved from Bridgeburg,

AT GRANDMOTHER'S.
the JELL-O hour.

Ontario to Montreal, Quebec. That same year, the **JELL-O** Company acquired Genesee Pudding Powder, a company which made vanilla, lemon, butterscotch and chocolate pudding mixes for the institutional market. In 1925, the Postum Company, acquired the **JELL-O** Company, forming the nucleus of what was to become The General Foods Company. **JELL-O** brand advertising in the 1920s included some of the most beautiful food illustrations ever created. Outstanding artists, such as Norman Rockwell, showed the ease of making **JELL-O** Jelly Powder with appealing family scenes, such as a little girl unmoulding a **JELL-O** treat for her doll and a grandmother making **JELL-O** desserts with her grandchildren. The flamboyance of the "Roaring Twenties" era was reflected in recipes like Peach Champagne Sparkle, Perfection Salad and Egg Slices en Gelée.

Salad Days Lead to Lime

Gelled or "congealed" salads became very popular in the late 1920s and early 1930s, with almost one-third of the salad recipes in the average cookbook gelatin-based. This led to the introduction of lime-flavoured **JELL-O** in 1930, a flavour well-suited to salads, appetizers, relishes and entrées. The advent of the automatic refrigerator gave the **JELL-O** brand a real boost, making it easier and twice as fast to create family favourites like Luncheon Salad and Plum Pudding and stylish geometrical dessert moulds reflecting the Art Deco age.

The Benny Era

"**JELL-O** again" became a familiar greeting over the radio air waves as Jack Benny, Mary Livingston, Don Wilson and the unforgettable **J-E-L-L-O** song brought **JELL-O** advertising into

▼ ▼ ▼

millions of homes every Sunday evening for ten years starting in 1934. In September 1936, Decca Records released "A Fine Romance," sung by Bing and Dixie Lee Crosby with Victor Young and his orchestra. Written by Dorothy Fields and Jerome Kern for the movie, "Swing Time," the number included the unforgettable words, "You take romance, I'll take **JELL-O.**"

JELL-O Brand Goes to War

During World War ll, Canadians made one-crusted pies as a way to save on shortening and sugar, which were in short supply. **JELL-O** Jelly Powder or pudding were perfect fillings for pies, since they offered rich flavour and very few additional ingredients were required.

Lighthearted '50s

No longer promoted as a food-stretcher, the **JELL-O** brand took a light-hearted approach, positioned as a treat and festive dessert in the 1950s. In 1953, **JELL-O** Instant Pudding was introduced in Canada with chocolate, vanilla and butterscotch flavours. Recognizing the dual use of its pudding products, General Foods decided to rename and promote this line as puddings and pie fillings in 1955. New **JELL-O** Jelly Powders — apple, grape, black cherry and black raspberry made their debut during this decade and in 1959, **JELL-O** brand began to offer larger family size packages for the popular red fruit flavours including strawberry, raspberry and cherry.

Joys of JELL-O

The '60s were a time of flavour expansion and experimentation for **JELL-O** Jelly Powder and **JELL-O** products and fruit was the promotion of the decade. The classic cookbook, *The Joys of*

JELL-O, was published in both English and French and has since gone through many printings and revisions, with book sales in the millions.

Faster is Better

With more and more women going to work and starting to feel pressured for time, "faster is better" became the **JELL-O** Jelly Powder thrust of the '70s. Consumers were offered shortcuts using ice cubes, frozen fruit, ice cream, a blender or an ice bath. Make ahead fruit and vegetable salads were promoted to complete the evening meal and parfait pies using **JELL-O,** ice cream and fresh fruit chilled in a pie crust became instantly popular, since they were so easy to make. In the late 1970s, the **"JELL-O** Tree" was a popular Canadian television campaign. The ads featured fruits representing **JELL-O** flavours and **JELL-O** packages hanging from a tree. Today, people still recall the tree and the line, "Hey, you kids, get out of that **JELL-O** tree!"

Cosby Speaks for JELL-O Jelly Powder

Bill Cosby joined the Canadian advertising efforts in 1980, beginning with the "Kids Love Pudding" campaign. Sales, which had been lackluster, began to turn around as baby boomers started families and served foods they loved as kids to their own children. The relationship between Cosby and the **JELL-O** brand continues to this day.

New Innovations for the '80s and '90s

JELL-O Jigglers* gelatin snacks were introduced in 1988, with the company's Consumer Response Center receiving 150 to 200 calls daily requesting the recipe for the colorful fingerfood snacks for kids. From Jigglers came **Snacktivities**, recipes that encouraged families to make fun recipes

▼ ▼ ▼ ▼ ▼ ▼

together using **JELL-O** Jelly Powder and Pudding. These exciting creations included fanciful edibles like Dirt Cups and No Drip Pops. Traditionally, blue has not been a big food colour, but today's kids think it's cool. Launched in 1992, Berry Blue sold 21 million packages in North America in its first year. In 1995, **JELL-O JELS**, ready-to-eat, shelf-stable snack cups were introduced and in the fall of 1995, Cranberry **JELL-O** Jelly Powder was launched, capitalizing on the growing popularity of cranberry flavour.

JELL-O in Space

In June 1996, the **JELL-O** brand made history in outer space. According to a Reuters dispatch, Shannon Lucid, an American astronaut on a 140-day mission to the Russian Mir space station, revealed that she kept track of time by allowing herself to eat **JELL-O** Jelly Powder on Sundays. After Lucid served her Russian crewmates their first **JELL-O** dessert as a special Easter treat, they decided to share a bag every Sunday night. "It is the greatest improvement in space flight, since my first flight over 10 years ago," Lucid wrote.

A new twist in 1997

Today, consumers love **JELL-O** Jelly Powder because it is a cool and refreshing fruity dessert or snack that the whole family can enjoy. It is quick and easy to make and fat free, as always. Scheduled to debut in July 1997 are new Tropical Twists **JELL-O** Jelly Powder flavours —Strawberry-Kiwi, Orange-Pineapple, Strawberry-Banana and Fruit Fiesta. (Fruit Fiesta will be available in both regular and light.) Almost every second in Canada, someone buys a package of **JELL-O** Jelly Powder, and that's why it has remained one of Canada's most famous desserts for 100 years.

*Kewpie Doll is a registered trademark of Cameo Doll Products Co., Inc.

TRICKS OF THE TRADE

For best results when preparing JELL-O Jelly Powder according to package directions, follow these easy guidelines.

1. To make a mixture that is clear and uniformly set, be sure the jelly is completely dissolved in boiling water or other boiling liquid before adding the cold liquid. Stirring with a rubber spatula will help ensure that all the crystals are dissolved.

2. To store prepared jelly overnight or longer, cover it to prevent drying.

3. To speed up chilling time, choose the right container. A metal bowl or mould will chill the jelly faster than glass. Individual servings in small moulds or serving dishes will chill more quickly than large servings.

4. The 30 Minute Set Method is a quick way to set jelly. Refer to directions on the package. Do not use this method for moulding jelly.

5. Avoid adding fresh or frozen pineapple, kiwi, mangos or papaya to jelly. They contain an enzyme that prevents jelly from setting.

6. For skinless cooked pudding, cool for 10 minutes after cooking, stir and place plastic wrap directly on surface of pudding. Chill for 30 minutes then stir and fill serving dishes. Serve warm or cold. By the way, warm pudding is extra delicious.

7. Try making jelly in the blender. Empty 1 pkg (85 g) JELL-O Jelly Powder into blender. Add 1 cup (250 mL) boiling water. Blend on low speed to dissolve jelly, about 30 seconds. Add 2 cups (500 mL) ice cubes. Blend at high speed until ice is melted. Chill in individual glasses 20 minutes. This forms a two layered dessert as it sets.

JELLY CHILLING TIME CHART

Use this chart as a guildine to determine the desired consistency and the approximate chilling time.

WHEN RECIPE SAYS:	IT MEANS JELLY SHOULD ...	SET TIME FOR REGULAR METHOD	SET TIME FOR 30 MINUTE SET METHOD	USE IT FOR
"Chill until slightly thickened"	Jelly should be consistency of unbeaten egg whites	1¼ hours	3 to 5 minutes	Adding creamy ingredients such as whipped topping, or when mixture will be beaten
"Chill until set but not firm"	Stick to the finger when touched and should mound or move to the side when bowl or mould is tilted	2 hours	30 minutes	Layering jelly mixture i.e. moulds
"Chill until firm"	Not stick to finger when touched and not mound or move when mould is tilted.	Individual moulds at least 3 hours 2 to 6 cup moulds at least 4 hours 8 to 12 cup moulds at least 5 hours or overnight		Unmoulding and serving

▼ ▼ ▼ ▼ ▼ ▼
THE SECRET TO MOULDING JELLY

THE MOULD

Use metal, plastic, square or round cake pans, fluted or plain tube pans, loaf pans, metal mixing bowls.

To determine the volume of the mould, measure first with water. Most recipes give an indication of the size of the mould needed.

For easier unmoulding, spray the mould with non-stick cooking spray before filling with jelly or brush lightly with vegetable oil.

Use less water in preparing jelly for moulding. For a 4-serving size package, reduce the cold water by ¼ cup (50 mL). The adjustment has already been made in recipes in this book.

To arrange fruits or vegetables in moulds, chill jelly until slightly thickened. Pour jelly into mould to about ¼-inch (.5 cm) depth. Arrange fruits or vegetables in decorative pattern in jelly. Chill until set but not firm, then pour remaining thickened jelly over pattern in mould.

To prevent spilling, place mould on tray in refrigerator before pouring in jelly.

TO UNMOULD, always allow jelly to set until firm by refrigerating several hours or overnight.

Moisten tips of fingers and gently pull jelly from around edge of mould. Or, use a small metal spatula or pointed knife dipped in warm water to loosen top edge.

Dip mould in warm, not hot, water, just to rim, for about 15 seconds. Lift from water, hold upright and shake to loosen jelly. Or, gently pull jelly from edge of mould.

Moisten chilled serving plate with water. (This allows jelly to be moved after unmoulding.) Place moistened serving plate on top of mould. Invert mould and plate; holding mould and plate together, shake slightly to loosen. Gently remove mould. If jelly does not release easily, dip mould in warm water again for a few seconds. Centre jelly on serving plate.

▼ ▼ ▼ ▼ ▼ ▼

OTHER PREPARATION TRICKS

Always dissolve jelly powder in boiling water, stirring for 2 minutes to be sure to dissolve all crystals. A rubber spatula works well to dissolve crystals.

For 30 Minute Set Method, dissolve 1 pkg (85g) JELL-O Jelly Powder in 1 cup (250 mL) boiling water. Add 2 cups (500 mL) ice cubes. Stir until jelly thickens, about 3 to 5 minutes. Remove only unmelted ice. Chill 30 minutes.

To flake jelly, prepare jelly as directed on package, reducing cold water to ¾ cup (175 mL). Pour into a shallow pan and chill until firm, about 2 hours. To flake, break jelly into small flakes with a fork and pile lightly into dishes, alone or with fruit or whipped topping.

To prepare jelly cubes, prepare jelly as above for flaking. Cut jelly into small cubes, using a sharp knife that has been dipped in hot water. To remove cubes from pan, quickly dip pan in warm water and remove with lifter. Serve in dishes with whipped topping or fruit, if desired.

To fold whipped topping into partially set jelly, use a rubber spatula and fold using an over and under motion, being careful not to 'mix' but to 'fold'. For a smooth mixture, be sure jelly is partially set, not too firm or your mixture will be lumpy.

To whip jelly, prepare jelly as directed on package. Chill until slightly thickened. Beat on high speed of electric mixer until light and fluffy, about 3 minutes. Or use 30 Minute Set Method, to 'slightly thickened' and beat as above.

▼ ▼ ▼

BERRY BLACK BEES

Prep time: 15 minutes   Chill time: 1 hour

1 pkg	(85 g) JELL-O Berry Black Jelly Powder	1 pkg
1 pkg	(4-serving size) JELL-O Vanilla Instant Pudding	1 pkg
10	Chocolate wafer cookies	10

Black shoestring licorice

▼ **PREPARE** jelly powder according to package directions, reducing cold water to ½ cup (125 mL); pour into shallow pan and chill until set, about 1 hr.

▼ **PREPARE** pudding according to package directions, reducing milk to 1½ cups (375 mL); chill 5 minutes.

▼ **TO MAKE** bees, break gelatin into small pieces using fork. Alternately layer gelatin and pudding in small plastic or glass cups, ending with pudding layer.

▼ **GARNISH** each bee with two chocolate wafer cookies for "wings", 1 black jelly candy for a "head" and 2 pieces of black shoestring licorice for "antennae".

MAKES 5 bees.

TIP: *For easy blending, use a wire whisk to blend pudding and milk.*

▼ ▼ ▼ ▼ ▼ ▼

BERRY BLUE SHOOTING STARS

Prep time: 10 minutes   Chill time: 30 minutes

1 cup	boiling water	250 mL
1 pkg	(85 g) JELL-O Berry Blue Jelly Powder	1 pkg
2 cups	ice cubes	500 mL
1 cup	thawed COOL WHIP Whipped Topping	250 mL
	Additional thawed COOL WHIP Whipped Topping	
4	marshmallows	4
	Coloured sugar	

▼ **ADD** boiling water to jelly powder. Stir until completely dissolved. Add ice cubes. Stir until jelly thickens (3 to 5 minutes). Remove any unmelted ice.

▼ **SPOON** thickened jelly into dessert dishes alternately with spoonfuls of whipped topping to form clouds. Refrigerate until set, about 30 minutes.

▼ **GARNISH** with additional whipped topping and marshmallows, cut into star shapes and sprinkled with coloured sugar.

MAKES 4 servings.

TIP: To cut marshmallows, flatten slightly with rolling pin and cut with star cutter. Moisten slightly with water and sprinkle with coloured sugar.

▼ ▼ ▼

SLUSHIES

Prep time: 5 minutes Freezing time: 4 hours or overnight

1 pkg	(85 g) JELL-O Jelly Powder, any flavour	1 pkg
1 cup	boiling water	250 mL
2 cups	ginger ale	500 mL

▼ **DISSOLVE** jelly powder in boiling water.

▼ **ADD** ginger ale and pour into an 8 inch (20 cm) square pan. Freeze until firm, 4 hours or overnight

▼ **TO SERVE,** use an ice cream scoop to fill serving dishes, paper cups or ice cream cones. Serve immediately.

MAKES 4 servings.

TIP: *Substitute your favourite carbonated beverage for the ginger ale. Serve with sliced fresh fruit, if desired.*

▼▼▼▼▼▼

BLOOMING BERRY FLOWERS

Prep time: 15 minutes   Chill time: 3 hours

2 pkg	(85 g **each**) JELL-O Strawberry Jelly Powder, or your favourite flavour	2 pkg
1¼ cups	boiling water	300 mL
4	paper cups (5 oz/147.8 mL each)	4
Flowers	Large marshmallows, coloured sprinkles, coloured coconut, candies, toothpicks, plastic straws cut in half.	

▼ **DISSOLVE** jelly powder in boiling water, stirring until completely dissolved, about 2 minutes. Pour into paper cups.

▼ **REFRIGERATE** until firm, at least 3 hours.

▼ **CUT** marshmallows into five pieces using scissors to make flower petals. Arrange petals in flower shape, pressing each petal tightly together. Press coloured sprinkles or coconut onto petals and candy for centre.

▼ **INSERT** toothpick through centre of marshmallow flowers. Place toothpick into straw.

▼ **CAREFULLY** peel away paper cups from jelly. Place on serving plate and insert flower straw in centre of pot.

MAKES 4 flower pots.

TIP: Be sure to press marshmallows together when freshly cut and still sticky, so they hold together well.

▼▼▼▼▼▼

CHOCOLATE PUDDING CATS

Prep time: 10 minutes

1 pkg	(4-serving size) JELL-O Chocolate Instant Pudding	1 pkg
2 cups	milk	500 mL
	Assorted candies: shoestring and assorted licorice, jelly beans, jujubes, etc.	

▼ **PREPARE** pudding according to package directions. Spoon into 4 round bowls. Let stand 5 minutes.

▼ **DECORATE** with candies to resemble cat faces.

MAKES 4 servings.

TIP: Use an assortment of fruit slices instead of candy to make face, i.e. banana slices, strawberry slices, mandarin oranges.

▼▼▼▼▼▼▼

COOKIE DUNK PUDDING

Prep time: 10 minutes

2 cups	cold milk	**500 mL**
1 pkg	(4-serving size) JELL-O Instant Pudding, any flavour	**1 pkg**
20-30	miniature cookies	**20-30**

▼ **POUR** milk into medium bowl. Add pudding mix. Beat at low speed with electric mixer or with wire whisk until well blended, 1 to 2 minutes. Let stand 5 minutes.

▼ **SPOON** half of the pudding into 4 dessert dishes. Stand 4 to 6 cookies in each dish of pudding, placing them along sides of dish. Top with remaining pudding.

▼ **SERVE** immediately or refrigerate until ready to serve. Garnish with a dollop of whipped topping and additional cookies, if desired.

MAKES 4 servings.

TIP: *If desired, break larger cookies into 4 pieces and substitute for the miniature cookies.*

▼▼▼▼▼▼

DIRT CUPS

Prep time: 10 minutes

1 pkg	(4-serving size) JELL-O Chocolate Instant Pudding	**1 pkg**
1 tub	(500 mL) thawed COOL WHIP Whipped Topping	**1 tub**
20	chocolate sandwich cookies, crushed ("dirt")	**20**
	Gummy worms	

▼ **PREPARE** pudding according to package directions.

▼ **FOLD** in whipped topping and half of crushed cookies.

▼ **TO ASSEMBLE,** place about 1 Tbsp (15 mL) crushed cookies in bottom of 6 dessert dishes. Fill dishes three-quarter full with pudding mixture. Top with remaining crushed cookies. Garnish with gummy worms.

▼ **CHILL** if not serving immediately.

MAKES 6 servings.

TIP: A fun idea for a kids party. Make in paper cups.

▼▼▼▼▼▼▼

ALASKAN PUDDING PIES

Prep time: 10 minutes   Freezing time: 3 hours

1 cup	cold milk	**250 mL**
1 pkg	(4-serving size) JELL-O Chocolate Instant Pudding, or your favourite flavour	**1 pkg**
2 cups	thawed COOL WHIP Whipped Topping	**500 mL**
36	large cookies, your favourite variety (chocolate chip, double chocolate)	**36**

▼ **COMBINE** milk and pudding mix; blend well. Fold into topping.

▼ **SPREAD** filling about ½-inch (1 cm) thick on half of the cookies. Top with remaining cookies, pressing lightly and smoothing around edges with knife.

▼ **FREEZE** until firm, about 3 hours. Store in covered container in freezer or wrap individually and store in freezer.

MAKES 18 snacks.

TIP: Add ½ cup (125 mL) chocolate chips or nuts to pudding mixture. Roll "pies" in chocolate chips or coloured sprinkles before freezing, if desired.

▼ ▼ ▼ ▼ ▼ ▼ ▼

FRUITY PIZZA FAVOURITES

Prep time: 15 minutes   Chill time: 3 hours or overnight

2 pkg	(85 g **each**) JELL-O Berry Black Jelly Powder	2 pkg
2 cups	boiling water	500 mL
1 cup	cold water	250 mL
	Thawed COOL WHIP Whipped Topping	
	Assortment of fresh fruit pieces for decoration	

▼ **DISSOLVE** jelly powder in boiling water, stirring until completely dissolved, about 2 minutes. Stir in cold water. Pour into 13 x 9 inch (33 x 23 cm) pan.

▼ **REFRIGERATE** until firm, 3 hours or overnight.

▼ **TO ASSEMBLE**, place about 4 inches (10 cm) of warm, **not hot**, water in sink. Dip pan in water just to top of pan for 5 seconds. Cut out circles using a 4 inch (10 cm) round cookie cutter or rim of a drinking glass. Lift carefully out of pan and place on serving plate.

▼ **SPOON** whipped topping onto centre of jelly, and spread to within ½-inch (1 cm) of edge.

▼ **DECORATE** with pieces of fruit.

MAKES 6 pizzas.

TIP: Use leftover jelly layered in dessert dishes, with whipped topping and fruit.

▼ ▼ ▼ ▼ ▼ ▼ ▼

JELL-O JIGGLERS

Prep time: 3 minutes   Chill time: 3 hours

2 pkg	(170 g **each**) JELL-O Jelly Powder, any flavour	2 pkg
	OR	
4 pkg	(85 g **each**) JELL-O Jelly Powder, any flavour	4 pkg
2½ **cups**	boiling water or boiling juice	625 mL

▼ **DISSOLVE** jelly powder in boiling water or boiling juice. Pour into 13 x 9 inch (33 x 23 cm) pan. Chill for 3 hours or until firm.

▼ **TO UNMOULD**, dip pan in warm water about 15 seconds. Cut into squares or use cookie cutters. Lift from pan. Store in refrigerator until needed.

MAKES about 24 jigglers.

TIP: *For easy dissolving of jelly powder, use a rubber spatula to stir and dissolve. This should take about 3 minutes.*

JELL-O MILK JIGGLERS

Prep time: 5 minutes   Chill time: 3 hours

4 pkg	(85 g **each**) JELL-O Jelly Powder, your favourite flavour	4 pkg
1 cup	boiling water	250 mL
1½ **cups**	milk	375 mL

▼ **DISSOLVE** jelly powder in boiling water. Cool to room temperature. Gradually stir in milk.

▼ **POUR** into 13 x 9 inch (33 x 23 cm) pan.

▼ **CHILL** for 3 hours or until firm.

▼ **TO UNMOULD**, dip pan in warm water about 15 seconds. Cut into squares or use cookie cutters. Lift from pan. Store in refrigerator until needed.

MAKES about 24 jigglers.

TIP: *For easy dissolving of jelly powder, use a rubber spatula to stir and dissolve. This should take about 3 minutes. Be sure to cool jelly down before adding milk or it will curdle.*

▼ ▼ ▼

▼ ▼ ▼ ▼ ▼ ▼ ▼

LOLLIPOP JIGGLES

Prep time: 10 minutes   Chill time: 3 hours

1¼ cups	boiling water	300 mL
2 pkg	(85 g **each**) JELL-O Jelly Powder, any flavour	2 pkg
4	small paper cups	4
6	plastic straws, cut in half	6

▼ **ADD** boiling water to jelly powder. Stir until completely dissolved. Let stand to cool for 15 minutes.

▼ **POUR** into paper cups. Refrigerate until firm at least 3 hours.

▼ **CAREFULLY** peel away cups. Using a knife dipped in warm water, cut each jelly cup horizontally into 3 round slices.

▼ **INSERT** straw half into each jelly slice to resemble a lollipop.

MAKES 12 pops.

> *TIP: Substitue ½ cup (125 mL) boiling fruit juice for ½ cup (125 mL) boiling water, if desired.*

▼ ▼ ▼ ▼ ▼ ▼ ▼

PUDDING FUN POPS

Prep time: 5 minutes   Freezing time: 4 hours or overnight

3 cups	milk	**750 mL**
1 pkg	(4-serving size) JELL-O Instant Pudding, any flavour	**1 pkg**
9	(3 oz / 85 mL) small paper cups	**9**
9	popsicle sticks	**9**

▼ **POUR** milk into a bowl. Add pudding to milk and beat with wire whisk until smooth, about 2 minutes.

▼ **SET** paper cups on cookie sheet. Pour pudding mixture into paper cups. Insert a popsicle stick into centre of each cup.

▼ **FREEZE** until firm, about 4 hours or overnight. If not using pops within 24 hours, store in a plastic bag. Dip pops in hot water for 10 seconds to unmould.

MAKES 9 pops.

VARIATION:

Make a S'More Pop! Place 3 or 4 miniature marshmallows and 1 tsp (5 mL) BAKER'S Miniature Chocolate Chips in bottom of each cup before filling with pudding.

TIP: *Use your favourite popsicle moulds instead of the cups.*

▼ ▼ ▼ ▼ ▼ ▼ ▼

Icy Blue Igloo

Prep time: 20 minutes   Chill time: 3 hours

3 pkg	(85 g **each**) JELL-O Berry Blue Jelly Powder	3 pkg
2¾ cups	boiling water	675 mL
1½ cups	cold water	375 mL
2 cups	ice cubes	500 mL
1 tub	(500 mL) thawed COOL WHIP Whipped Topping	1 tub

▼ **DISSOLVE** 2 packages of jelly powder in 2 cups (500 mL) boiling water. Add cold water. Pour into 13 x 9 inch (33 x 23 cm) pan. Chill until set, about 3 hours. Cut jelly into ½ inch (1 cm) cubes. Set aside.

▼ **LINE** a 6 cup (1.5 L) bowl with plastic wrap. Set aside.

▼ **DISSOLVE** remaining package of jelly powder in ¾ cup (175 mL) boiling water. Add ice cubes. Stir until slightly thickened, about 3 to 5 minutes. Remove any unmelted ice. Whisk in 1 cup (250 mL) whipped topping. Stir in ⅔ of the jelly cubes and pour mixture into prepared bowl. Chill until set, about 3 hours.

▼ **UNMOULD** onto serving plate. Remove plastic wrap and frost surface with remaining whipped topping and decorate with remaining jelly cubes.

MAKES 8 servings.

TIP: To make 4 individual igloos, divide jelly mixture between 4 small bowls lined with plastic wrap and continue as directed above. The kids can have some fun and frost and decorate their own igloo.

▼ ▼ ▼

▼ ▼ ▼ ▼ ▼ ▼ ▼

Squisharoos

Prep time: 5 minutes

1 pkg	(85 g) JELL-O Jelly Powder, any flavour	1 pkg
24	large marshmallows	24

▼ **EMPTY** jelly powder into a large plastic bag.

▼ **MOISTEN** marshmallows with water and shake 3 or 4 at a time in jelly powder to coat.

MAKES about two dozen.

TIP: *If desired, cut marshmallows into fun shapes by flattening slightly and cutting with small cutters.*

▼ ▼ ▼ ▼ ▼ ▼ ▼

SUPER NO-DRIP POPS

Prep time: 5 minutes   Freezing time: 3 hours or overnight

1 pkg	(85 g) JELL-O Jelly Powder, any flavour	**1 pkg**
1 pouch	(135 g) KOOL-AID Sugar-Sweetened Drink Mix, any flavour	**1 pouch**
2 cups	boiling water	**500 mL**
1½ cups	cold water	**375 mL**
11	(3 oz/85 mL) paper cups	**11**
11	popsicle sticks	**11**

▼ **DISSOLVE** jelly powder and drink mix in boiling water. Add cold water.

▼ **SET** paper cups on cookie sheet. Pour jelly mixture into paper cups.

▼ **FREEZE** until partially set, about 2 hours.

▼ **INSERT** a popsicle stick into centre of each cup. Freeze until firm.

MAKES about 11 pops.

TIPS: Use your own popsicle containers, if desired.

Substitute fruit juice for the cold water, if desired.

▼ ▼ ▼ ▼ ▼ ▼

TREASURE CHESTS

Prep time: 15 minutes   Chill time: 3 hours or overnight

2 pkg	(85 g **each**) JELL-O Berry Black Jelly Powder	**2 pkg**
2 cups	boiling water	**500 mL**
1 cup	cold water	**250 mL**
	Thawed COOL WHIP Whipped Topping	
	Candies, Chocolate Wafers for decorations	

▼ **DISSOLVE** jelly powder in boiling water, stirring until completely dissolved, about 2 minutes. Stir in cold water. Pour into 8 x 4 inch (20 x 12 cm) loaf pan.

▼ **REFRIGERATE** until firm, 3 hours or overnight.

▼ **DIP** cake pan in warm water just to top of pan for 5 seconds. Unmould onto board.

▼ **DIVIDE** jelly into 4 equal treasure chests. Cut a small section from centre of each chest, leaving a 1 inch (2.5 cm) border.

▼ **FILL** cavity with whipped topping and candies. Use 2 chocolate wafers for lid of each treasure chest.

MAKES 4 treasure chests.

> **TIP:** Use fruit pieces instead of candies, if desired.

▼ ▼ ▼ ▼ ▼ ▼

WATERMELON PIT PARFAIT

Prep time: 10 minutes   Chill time: 30 minutes

2 cups	thawed COOL WHIP Whipped Topping	**500 mL**
5 drops	green food colouring	**5 drops**
1 cup	boiling water	**250 mL**
1 pkg	(85 g) JELL-O Wiggly Watermelon Jelly Powder	**1 pkg**
2 cups	ice cubes	**500 mL**
2 Tbsp	BAKER'S Miniature Semi-Sweet Chocolate Chips	**25 mL**

▼ **MIX** whipped topping with food colouring. Spread green topping evenly inside 4 dessert dishes to make "rind". Place in freezer while preparing jelly.

▼ **ADD** boiling water to jelly powder. Stir until completely dissolved. Add ice cubes. Stir until slightly thickened, 3 to 5 minutes. Remove any unmelted ice. Spoon into prepared dessert dishes.

▼ **POKE** chocolate chips into jelly to make "seeds". Chill 30 minutes.

MAKES 4 desserts.

TIP: *For best results, use a rubber spatula when dissolving jelly powder in boiling water.*

▼ ▼ ▼ ▼ ▼ ▼

WIGGLY BANANA SPLITS

Prep time: 15 minutes   Chill time: 3 hours

1 pkg	(85 g) JELL-O Wiggly Watermelon or Strawberry-Kiwi Jelly Powder	1 pkg
1 cup	boiling water	250 mL
¾ cup	cold water	175 mL
1 pkg	(4-serving size) JELL-O Vanilla Instant Pudding	1 pkg
4	small bananas, peeled and sliced lengthwise	4
1 cup	thawed COOL WHIP Whipped Topping	250 mL
4	maraschino cherries	4

▼ **DISSOLVE** jelly powder in boiling water. Add cold water. Pour into an 8 inch (20 cm) square pan. Refrigerate until firm, about 3 hours.

▼ **PREPARE** pudding as directed on package.

▼ **CUT** jelly into small cubes. Place a few cubes on bottom of each dish. Top with some of the pudding.

▼ **TOP** with sliced bananas, more pudding, cubes, whipped topping and cherries.

MAKES 4 servings.

TIP: *Dip bananas in lemon juice to prevent browning.*

▼ ▼ ▼

WIGGLY WATERMELON WORMS

Prep time: 10 minutes   Chill time: 45 minutes

1 pkg	(85 g) JELL-O Wiggly Watermelon Jelly Powder	1 pkg
½ cup	warm water	125 mL
1½ cups	miniature marshmallows	375 mL
4	chocolate wafer cookies, crushed ("dirt", optional)	4
	Black shoestring licorice	

▼ **SPRAY** a 8 or 9 inch (20 or 23 cm) square pan with a non-stick cooking spray. Spread on bottom and sides of pan with paper towel.

▼ **MIX** jelly powder and warm water in medium microwavable bowl.

▼ **MICROWAVE** on HIGH 1½ minutes. Stir to dissolve completely.

▼ **ADD** marshmallows and microwave on HIGH 1 minute or until marshmallows are puffed and almost melted. Stir mixture slowly until marshmallows are completely melted and mixture is smooth. (Creamy layer will float to top.)

▼ **POUR** into prepared pan. Refrigerate 45 minutes or until set. Loosen edges with knife. Cut into 16, ½ inch (1 cm) strips.

▼ **SNIP** licorice into small pieces for eyes and attach to "worms."

▼ **SPRINKLE** cookie crumbs on a plate to resemble dirt. Place "Worms" on top of dirt.

MAKES 16 pieces.

TIP: These "worms" can be made with any flavour of JELL-O. They may also be made in a saucepan on top of the stove. Combine jelly powder and warm water in a saucepan over medium heat. Stir to dissolve, about 2 minutes, stir in marshmallows and heat until melted, about 2 minutes. Remove and proceed as above.

RAZZLE DAZZLE BERRY MOUSSE

Prep time: 10 minutes   Chill time: 10 minutes

1 pkg	(85 g) JELL-O Strawberry Jelly Powder	1 pkg
1 cup	boiling water	250 mL
1 pkg	(300 g) frozen unsweetened strawberries	1 pkg
1½ cups	thawed COOL WHIP Whipped Topping	375 mL

▼ **DISSOLVE** jelly powder in boiling water. Add frozen strawberries, breaking apart with a fork. Stir until slightly thickened, 3 to 5 minutes.

▼ **FOLD** in whipped topping. Pour into dessert dishes. Chill 10 minutes.

MAKES 6 servings.

TIP: *For Raspberry Mousse, use 1 pkg (85 g) JELL-O Raspberry Jelly Powder and 1 pkg (300 g) frozen unsweetened raspberries.*

CITRUS MERINGUE

Prep time: 10 minutes   Chill time: 10 minutes

1 pkg	(85 g) JELL-O Lemon or Orange-Pineapple Jelly Powder	1 pkg
1½ cups	peeled and chopped orange and grapefruit segments	375 mL

▼ **PREPARE** jelly powder according to 30 Minute Set Method on package.

▼ **SET ASIDE** ⅔ cup (150 mL) of slightly thickened jelly. Stir fruit into remaining jelly; spoon into 4 dessert dishes.

▼ **BEAT** reserved jelly with electric mixer until double in volume. Spoon over fruited layer in dishes. Chill until set, about 10 minutes.

MAKES 4 servings.

TIP: *For best results when beating jelly - it must be of egg white consistency before beating.*

DID YOU KNOW HOW TO PEEL AND SEGMENT CITRUS FRUITS:

Cut off both ends of fruit. Cut the skin working down the rounded slope of the fruit, cutting off both pith and peel. Hold peeled fruit and slice down between membranes to free each segment.

▼▼▼▼▼▼

CREAMY MOUSSE DELIGHT

Prep time: 10 minutes   Chill time: 30 minutes

1 pkg	(4-serving size) JELL-O Instant Pudding, any flavour	**1 pkg**
1 tub	(500 mL) thawed COOL WHIP or COOL WHIP Light Whipped Topping	**1 tub**

▼ **PREPARE** pudding as directed on package.

▼ **FOLD** in whipped topping.

▼ **SPOON** into individual dessert dishes. Chill about 30 minutes.

MAKES 6 servings.

TIP: Fold in 1 (40 to 50 g) chopped chocolate bar of your choice.

FRUITY SHAKES

Prep time: 10 minutes

½ cup	boiling water	**125 mL**
1 pkg	(85 g) JELL-O Berry Blue Jelly Powder	**1 pkg**
2 cups	vanilla ice cream	**500 mL**
1 cup	milk	**250 mL**
½ cup	crushed ice	**125 mL**

▼ **POUR** water in electric blender container. Add jelly powder. Cover and blend at medium speed for 1 minute. Scrape sides of container.

▼ **WITH** machine running, add ice cream by spoonfuls through hole in lid of blender.

▼ **ADD** milk and ice; blend at medium speed for 30 seconds. Serve immediately.

MAKES 3 to 4 servings.

TIP: Use any flavour of jelly powder and add ½ cup (125 mL) fruit to the blender with the ice cream, if desired.

DID YOU KNOW ABOUT FROZEN FRUIT:

For maximum freshness, use in 3 months. Do not hold longer than 6 months. Do not refreeze thawed fruit. To thaw fruit, place unopened package in bowl. Allow to stand at room temperature for 2½ hours.

Opposite page: Citrus Meringue, Razzle Dazzle Berry Mousse, Creamy Mousse Delight

Above: Fruity Shakes

QUICK AND EASY BUTTERSCOTCH FUDGE

Prep time: 10 minutes   Chill time: 1 hour

¼ cup	milk	50 mL
1 pkg	(6-serving size) JELL-O Butterscotch Pudding and Pie Filling	1 pkg
3 Tbsp	butter	45 mL
2¼ cups	sifted icing sugar	525 mL
⅔ cup	chopped nuts	150 mL

▼ **LINE** a small loaf pan with waxed paper.

▼ **BLEND** milk gradually into pudding mix in a medium microwavable bowl. Add butter.

▼ **COOK** uncovered on HIGH power for 1 minute. Stir well. Cook on HIGH power for 1 minute. Mixture should just start to foam or boil around the edges. Do not overcook. Stir well.

▼ **QUICKLY** blend in icing sugar and nuts.

▼ **POUR** into pan and chill 45 minutes to one hour. Cut into pieces. Store in refrigerator.

MAKES 18 to 24 pieces.

NOTE: Tested in 700 watt oven. For 500 watt oven increase second cooking time to 65 seconds.

TIP: *Use JELL-O Chocolate or Vanilla Pudding and Pie Filling, if desired. Add ½ cup (125 mL) dried fruit such as apricots, cranberries or candied cherries, if desired.*

Above: Quick and Easy Butterscotch Fudge

▼ ▼ ▼

▼ ▼ ▼ ▼ ▼ ▼ ▼

CREAMY DELIGHT CUPS

Prep time: 15 minutes   Chill time: 30 minutes

1 pkg	(85 g) JELL-O Jelly Powder, any flavour	1 pkg
1 cup	boiling water	250 mL
2 cups	vanilla ice cream	500 mL

▼ **DISSOLVE** jelly powder in boiling water. Cool in refrigerator for about 10 minutes.

▼ **WHISK** in ice cream.

▼ **POUR** into individual dessert dishes, chill until set, about 30 minutes.

MAKES 6 servings.

TIP: Adding ice cream makes this recipe set in 30 minutes. Be creative with your favourite ice cream and JELL-O flavours. Substitute frozen yogurt for ice cream, if desired.

QUICK AND EASY FLUFFY MOUSSE

Prep time: 15 minutes   Chill time: 1 hour

1 pkg	(85 g) JELL-O Jelly Powder, any flavour	1 pkg
1 tub	(500 mL) thawed COOL WHIP or COOL WHIP Light Whipped Topping	1 tub

▼ **PREPARE** jelly powder according to 30 Minute Set Method on package.

▼ **REMOVE** any unmelted ice cubes, fold in whipped topping.

▼ **CHILL** until set, about 1 hour.

MAKES 6 servings.

TIP: Add ½ cup (125 mL) sliced fruit after removing ice cubes, if desired.

JUICY JELLY CUPS

Prep time: 10 minutes   Chill time: 1 hour

1 pkg	(85 g) JELL-O Jelly Powder, any flavour	1 pkg
1 cup	fruit juice	250 mL

▼ **PREPARE** jelly powder with 1 cup (250 mL) boiling water. Stir in fruit juice in place of cold water.

▼ **CHILL** in individual dessert dishes until set, about 1 hour.

MAKES 4 servings.

TIP: Use JELL-O Strawberry Jelly Powder and apple juice or JELL-O Cranberry Jelly Powder with orange or raspberry juice or experiment with your own flavour combo.

▼ ▼ ▼

Juicy Jelly Cups
add fruit juice

Jelly Sparkle
add carbonated beverage

Quick and Easy
Fluffy Mousse
add whipped topping

Jelly Smoothy
add yogurt

Jelly Cow
add milk

Creamy Delight Cups
add ice cream

IT'S SO QUICK AND EASY
WITH JELL-O

By simply adding thawed COOL WHIP Whipped Topping, fruit juice, carbonated beverages, ice cream, milk and yogurt to JELL-O Jelly Powder you can create fun desserts that your whole family will love. See pages 38 and 40.

Above: Quick and Easy JELL-O Desserts

▼ ▼ ▼ ▼ ▼ ▼

JELLY SMOOTHY

Prep time: 15 minutes   Chill time: 30 minutes

1 pkg	(85 g) JELL-O Jelly Powder, any flavour	**1 pkg**
1 cup	boiling water	**250 mL**
2 cups	plain or fruit yogurt or frozen vanilla yogurt	**500 mL**

▼ **DISSOLVE** jelly powder in boiling water. Cool in refrigerator for about 10 minutes .

▼ **WHISK** in yogurt.

▼ **PLACE** in refrigerator and chill until set, about 30 minutes.

Makes 4 servings.

TIP: Make sure water has just boiled for best dissolving of jelly powder.

JELLY COW

Prep time: 15 minutes   Chill time: 1 hour

1 pkg	(85 g) JELL-O Jelly Powder, any flavour	**1 pkg**
1 cup	boiling water	**250 mL**
2 cups	milk	**500 mL**

▼ **DISSOLVE** jelly powder in boiling water. Cool to room temperature.

▼ **GRADUALLY** stir in milk. Pour into dessert dishes.

▼ **CHILL** until set, about 1 hour.

MAKES 6 servings.

TIP: Cooling the jelly is very important or the milk will curdle.

JELLY SPARKLE

Prep time: 5 minutes   Chill time: 3 hours

1 pkg	(85 g) JELL-O Jelly Powder, any flavour	**1 pkg**
1 cup	boiling water	**250 mL**
1 cup	cold carbonated beverage	**250 mL**

▼ **DISSOLVE** jelly powder in boiling water. Cool to room temperature.

▼ **ADD** carbonated beverage and chill in dessert dishes until set, about 3 hours.

MAKES 4 servings.

SUGGESTED COMBINATIONS:

- Lime jelly powder with ginger ale.
- Orange jelly powder with root beer.
- Cherry jelly powder with cola.

TIP: Cool down the jelly mixture until room temperature before adding the carbonated beverage if you wish to maintain the carbonation.

▼ ▼ ▼

CREATE-A-PUDDING SNACK

Prep time: 10 minutes   Chill time: 30 minutes

1 pkg	(4-serving size) JELL-O Instant Pudding, any flavour	1 pkg
½ cup	mini or crumbled cookies, crushed fruit, mini-marshmallows	125 mL

▼ **PREPARE** pudding as directed on package.

▼ **STIR** in cookies, fruit or marshmallows.

▼ **SPOON** into individual dessert dishes. Chill 30 minutes.

MAKES 6 servings.

TIP: *A fun party idea. Let the kids make their own.*

Above: Create-A-Pudding Snack

▼ ▼ ▼ ▼ ▼ ▼

FUN AND EASY PUDSICLES

Prep time: 5 minutes   Freezing time: 4 hours or overnight

JELL-O Pudding or Jels Snacks, any flavour

▼ **INSERT** spoon or popsicle stick through foil cover of pudding or jels.

▼ **FREEZE** until firm, about 4 hours or overnight. Peel away foil top. Run warm water over popsicles for a few seconds to loosen plastic container.

▼ **DIP** in toppings of your choice, if desired or eat plain.

TIP: *Remove foil lid and stir in jam, chopped candy bars or chopped cookies. Place stick in cup and freeze. If desired, remove stick and container after freezing, and cover with thawed COOL WHIP Whipped Topping for a quick dessert.*

Above: Fun and Easy Pudsicles

▼ ▼ ▼

FUN AND EASY SNACK CUPS

Prep time: 5 minutes

JELL-O Pudding Snacks, any flavour

▼ **STIR** chopped fruit, such as bananas or stawberries into your favourite snack cup flavour just before serving.

▼ **STIR** chocolate chips, chopped or mini cookies, chopped candy bars, mini marshmallows or sprinkles into your favourite snack cup flavour just before serving.

> **TIP:** *Create your own pudding snack—use your imagination.*

Above: Fun and Easy Snack Cups

DESSERT EXPRESS

JELL-O Pudding Snacks, any flavour

▼ **EASY FONDUE:** Heat 1 pudding snack in microwave oven on medium power for 1 minute or until warm. Serve with a selection of fruit, marshmallows and cake.

▼ **EASY MOUSSE:** Fold ½ cup (125 mL) thawed COOL WHIP Whipped Topping into 1 chocolate pudding snack. Spoon into serving dish.

MAKES 1 serving.

▼ **ICY PUDDING TREAT:** Serve your favourite flavour of pudding with your favourite flavour of ice cream for a taste sensation.

TIP: Give your kids a separate bag with pudding 'stir-ins' for their lunch.

*Above: Easy Fondue, Easy Mousse,
Icy Pudding Treat*

PEANUT BUTTER AND GRAPE JELLY PIE

Prep time: 50 minutes   Chill time: 3 hours or overnight

1 cup	milk	**250 mL**
½ cup	KRAFT Smooth Peanut Butter	**125 mL**
1 pkg	(4-serving size) JELL-O Vanilla Instant Pudding	**1 pkg**
2½ cups	thawed COOL WHIP Whipped Topping, divided	**625 mL**
1	prepared 9 inch (23 cm) graham wafer crumb crust	**1**
1 pkg	(85 g) JELL-O Giggly Grape Jelly Powder	**1 pkg**
¾ cup	boiling water	**175 mL**
2 cups	ice cubes	**500 mL**

▼ **STIR** milk gradually into peanut butter in medium bowl until smooth. Add pudding mix. Beat with wire whisk until smooth, about 2 minutes. Gently stir in 1 cup (250 mL) whipped topping.

▼ **SPOON** mixture into bottom of crumb crust. Refrigerate.

▼ **DISSOLVE** jelly powder in boiling water. Add ice cubes and stir until slightly thickened, about 3 to 5 minutes. Remove any unmelted ice. Whisk in remaining whipped topping. Chill until mixture is slightly thickened, about 30 minutes.

▼ **SPOON** mixture onto peanut butter mixture in crumb crust. Refrigerate 3 hours or overnight.

MAKES 8 servings.

TIP: Freeze pie overnight, if desired. Let stand on counter 10 minutes before serving.

DID YOU KNOW ABOUT KRAFT PEANUT BUTTER:

There are 6 types of peanut butter in the KRAFT line up—from Extra Creamy to Crunchy. Use the one of your choice. Did you know that 2 Tbsp (25 mL) of peanut butter contains 6.5 g of protein. It's also a good source of folacin plus niacin and thiamine.

▼▼▼

▼ ▼ ▼ ▼ ▼ ▼

CHOCOLATE CANDY BAR DESSERT

Prep time: 20 minutes   Chill time: 2 hours

2 cups	chocolate wafer crumbs	**500 mL**
½ cup	butter, melted	**125 mL**
1 pkg	(250 g) PHILADELPHIA Cream Cheese, softened	**1 pkg**
¼ cup	granulated sugar	**50 mL**
1 tub	(1 L) thawed COOL WHIP Whipped Topping	**1 tub**
1 cup	chopped chocolate-covered crisp butter toffee bars (about 5 bars)	**250 mL**
3 cups	cold milk	**750 mL**
2 pkg	(4-serving size **each**) JELL-O Chocolate Instant Pudding	**2 pkg**

▼ **COMBINE** crumbs with butter. Press firmly onto bottom of 13 x 9 inch (33 x 23 cm) baking pan. Chill.

▼ **MIX** cream cheese and sugar in medium bowl with electric mixer until smooth. Gently stir in ½ of the whipped topping. Spread evenly over crust. Sprinkle chopped candy bars over cream cheese layer.

▼ **POUR** milk into a large bowl. Add pudding mixes. Beat with wire whisk on low speed of electric mixer for 2 minutes. Pour over chopped candy bar layer. Let stand 5 minutes or until thickened.

▼ **SPREAD** remaining whipped topping over pudding layer.

▼ **REFRIGERATE** 2 hours or until firm. Garnish with additional chopped candy bars, if desired. Cut into squares. Store leftover dessert in refrigerator.

MAKES 15 to 18 servings.

TIP: For easy chopping of candy bars, leave in wrapper and break gently with the "handle" of a knife.

RASPBERRY SMOOTHIE

Prep time: 5 minutes   Chill time: 15 minutes

1 pkg	(85 g) JELL-O Raspberry Jelly Powder	**1 pkg**
1 cup	boiling water	**250 mL**
2 cups	vanilla ice cream	**500 mL**

▼ **DISSOLVE** jelly powder in boiling water.

▼ **ADD** ice cream by spoonfuls, whisking until smooth. Chill 15 minutes, or until mixture is slightly thickened.

▼ **SPOON** into dessert dishes.

▼ **CHILL** until set.

MAKES 4 servings.

TIP: Serve with fresh raspberries, if desired.

Opposite page: Peanut Butter and Grape Jelly Pie, Chocolate Candy Bar Dessert

AMBROSIA PARFAIT

Prep time: 20 minutes   Chill time: 30 minutes

1 pkg	(4-serving size) JELL-O Vanilla Instant Pudding	1 pkg
1 cup	cold milk	250 mL
1 cup	crushed pineapple, undrained	250 mL
1	small banana, chopped	1
1 cup	miniature marshmallows	250 mL
1 can	(10 oz/284 mL) mandarin orange sections, drained	1 can
½ cup	sliced almonds, toasted	125 mL
½ cup	BAKER'S ANGEL FLAKE Coconut	125 mL

▼ **PREPARE** pudding as directed on package reducing milk to 1 cup (250 mL).

▼ **STIR IN** pineapple, banana and ½ cup (125 mL) of the marshmallows.

▼ **SPOON** one-third of the pudding mixture into 6 parfait glasses. Layer remaining ingredients, alternating with layers of pudding.

▼ **CHILL** until ready to serve, about 30 minutes.

MAKES 6 servings.

TIP: Substitute 2 peeled and sectioned (membranes removed) fresh oranges for the mandarins, if desired.

Above: Ambrosia Parfait, Raspberry Smoothie

Mocha Chocolate Delight Pie

Prep time: 15 minutes   Cooking time: 10 minutes   Chill time: 3 hours

1 pkg	(6-serving size) JELL-O Chocolate Pudding and Pie Filling	1 pkg
2 tsp	instant coffee granules	10 mL
1	prepared 9 inch (23 cm) graham wafer crumb crust	1
1 tub	(500 mL) thawed COOL WHIP Whipped Topping	1 tub

▼ **PREPARE** pudding and pie filling as directed on package; stir in coffee. Cool 5 minutes, stirring twice.

▼ **MEASURE** 1 cup (250 mL) pudding; cover with waxed paper. Chill until cool, about ½ hour.

▼ **SPOON** remaining pie filling into crumb crust. Cover with waxed paper. Chill.

▼ **BEAT** measured filling until smooth; fold into 1½ cups (375 mL) whipped topping. Spread over filling in crumb crust. Chill 3 hours. Garnish with remaining whipped topping.

MAKES 8 servings.

TIP: Eliminate coffee and substitute 1 Tbsp (15 mL) grated orange rind, if desired.

Above from left to right: Rocky Road & Cookies'n Cream Ice Cream Shop Pies, Mocha Chocolate Delight Pie

▼ ▼ ▼

▼ ▼ ▼ ▼ ▼ ▼

COOKIES'N CREAM ICE CREAM SHOP PIE

Prep time: 15 minutes   Freezing time: 6 hours or overnight

1½ cups	cold milk or half and half cream	375 mL
1 pkg	(4-serving size) JELL-O Vanilla Instant Pudding	1 pkg
3½ cups	thawed COOL WHIP Whipped Topping	875 mL
1 cup	chopped chocolate sandwich cookies	250 mL
1	prepared 9 inch (23 cm) graham wafer crumb crust	1

▼ **POUR** milk into large bowl. Add pudding mix. Beat with wire whisk until well blended, 1 to 2 minutes. Let stand 5 minutes or until slightly thickened.

▼ **FOLD** whipped topping and chopped cookies into pudding mixture. Spoon into crumb crust.

▼ **FREEZE** pie until firm, about 6 hours or overnight. Remove from freezer. Let stand at room temperature about 10 minutes before serving to soften. Store any leftover pie in freezer.

MAKES 8 servings.

TIP: For a lighter version, use JELL-O Light Instant Pudding and COOL WHIP Light Whipped Topping. If desired, chill pie for 3 hours and serve.

ROCKY ROAD ICE CREAM SHOP PIE

Prep time: 15 minutes   Freezing time: 6 hours or overnight

1½ cups	cold milk or half and half cream	375 mL
1 pkg	(4-serving size) JELL-O Chocolate Instant Pudding	1 pkg
3½ cups	thawed COOL WHIP Whipped Topping	875 mL
½ cup	**each** BAKER'S Semi-Sweet Chocolate Chips, miniature marshmallows and chopped nuts	125 mL
1	prepared 9 inch (23 cm) chocolate wafer crumb crust	1

▼ **POUR** milk into large bowl. Add pudding mix. Beat with wire whisk until well blended, 1 to 2 minutes. Let stand 5 minutes or until slightly thickened.

▼ **FOLD** whipped topping, chocolate chips, marshmallows and nuts into pudding mixture. Spoon into crumb crust.

▼ **FREEZE** pie until firm, about 6 hours or overnight. Remove from freezer. Let stand at room temperature about 10 minutes before serving to soften. Store leftover pie in freezer.

MAKES 8 servings.

TIP: For best results when folding, use a rubber spatula. If desired, chill pie for 3 hours and serve.

▼ ▼ ▼

ORANGES TO GO

Prep time: 15 minutes   Chill time: 30 minutes

4	large oranges	4
1 pkg	(85 g) JELL-O Juicy Orange Jelly Powder	**1 pkg**
1 cup	boiling water	**250 mL**
2 cups	vanilla ice cream	**500 mL**

▼ **CUT** oranges in half. Remove fruit from each half. Scrape shells clean with a metal spoon. Finely chop fruit, removing membrane and set aside.

▼ **DISSOLVE** jelly powder in boiling water. Add ice cream by spoonfuls, stirring until smooth.

▼ **CHILL** until mixture is slightly thickened, about 15 minutes. Fold in chopped fruit.

▼ **SPOON** into orange shells. Chill until set, about 30 minutes.

MAKES 8 servings.

> ***TIP:*** *Use fresh orange juice for the boiling liquid, if desired.*

Above: Oranges To Go

Above: Microwave Apple Bread Pudding,
Dessert Nachos

▼ ▼ ▼ ▼ ▼ ▼

MICROWAVE APPLE BREAD PUDDING

Prep time: 5 minutes   Microwave cooking time: 13 minutes

6	slices raisin bread	6
2½ cups	milk	**625 mL**
1 pkg	(6-serving size) JELL-O Vanilla Pudding and Pie Filling	**1 pkg**
2	eggs, beaten	**2**
½ cup	raisins	**125 mL**
2	medium apples, peeled and chopped	**2**
¼ cup	packed brown sugar	**50 mL**
½ tsp	ground cinnamon	**2 mL**

▼ **CUT** bread into ½ inch (1 cm) cubes and set aside.

▼ **GRADUALLY WHISK** milk into pudding mix in a large microwavable bowl.

▼ **COOK** on HIGH power for 5 minutes, stirring twice. Add eggs, stirring well and continue to cook on HIGH power another 3 minutes, stirring once.

▼ **STIR** in raisins and apples. Cook 4 minutes more stirring once. Gently stir in bread cubes and cook another minute.

▼ **BLEND** sugar and cinnamon. Sprinkle over pudding. Serve warm.

MAKES 6 to 8 servings.

TIP: Use white bread, if desired.

DESSERT NACHOS

Prep time: 20 minutes

20	graham wafers	20
1 pkg	(4-serving size) JELL-O Vanilla Instant Pudding	**1 pkg**
2 cups	strawberries, sliced	**500 mL**
3	kiwi, chopped	**3**
1	large banana, sliced	**1**
	Chocolate sauce	

▼ **SCORE** each graham wafer diagonally with knife; break apart to form 2 triangles.

▼ **PREPARE** pudding as directed on package.

▼ **DIVIDE** graham wafer triangles evenly among 8 dessert plates. Spoon pudding over the triangles. Top with fruit.

▼ **DRIZZLE** with chocolate sauce. Serve immediately.

MAKES 8 servings.

TIP: Create your own flavour combination of pudding and fruit as desired. A fun party idea. Have all components made and let people create their own "nachos".

▼ ▼ ▼

▼ ▼ ▼ ▼ ▼ ▼

STRIPE IT RICH

Prep time: 30 minutes   Baking time: 20 minutes   Chill time: 2 to 3 hours

1¼ cups	all-purpose flour	**300 mL**
¾ cup	finely chopped pecans	**175 mL**
½ cup	granulated sugar, divided	**125 mL**
½ cup	butter, melted	**125 mL**
1 pkg	(250 g) PHILADELPHIA Cream Cheese, softened	**1 pkg**
3 cups	cold milk, divided	**750 mL**
1 tub	(1 L) thawed COOL WHIP Whipped Topping	**1 tub**
2 pkg	(4-serving size **each**) JELL-O Chocolate Instant Pudding	**2 pkg**

Chocolate curls (optional)

▼ **COMBINE** flour, pecans, ¼ cup (50 mL) of the sugar and butter until moist. Press mixture evenly into bottom of 13 x 9 inch (33 x 23 cm) pan. Bake at 350°F (180°C) for 20 minutes or until lightly golden. Cool on rack.

▼ **BEAT** cream cheese with remaining ¼ cup (50 mL) sugar and 2 Tbsp (25 mL) of the milk until smooth. Fold in half of the topping. Spread over cooled crust.

▼ **POUR** the remaining milk into a large bowl. Add pudding mixes. Beat with wire whisk until well blended, about 2 to 3 minutes scraping bowl occasionally. Pour over cream cheese layer. Chill 2 to 3 hours.

▼ **CUT** into servings and garnish each with the remaining topping. Add chocolate curls, if desired.

MAKES 16 servings.

TIP: Dessert may be frozen for up to 1 week. Thaw in refrigerator.

DID YOU KNOW ABOUT COOL WHIP WHIPPED TOPPING:

COOL WHIP comes in Regular or Light (low in fat). Both products may be interchanged in these recipes, if desired. Remember, COOL WHIP Whipped Topping may be re-frozen if your recipe doesn't use the entire container or use it to top your favourite dessert.

▼ ▼ ▼

CHOCOLATE WAFER-ORANGE DESSERT

Prep time: 15 minutes   Chill time: 3 hours or overnight

18	chocolate wafers	18
1 pkg	(4-serving size) JELL-O Vanilla Instant Pudding	1 pkg
1 cup	milk	250 mL
1 cup	thawed COOL WHIP Whipped Topping	250 mL
2	medium oranges, peeled and thinly sliced	2
3 Tbsp	orange marmalade	45 mL
1 tsp	water	5 mL

▼ **ARRANGE** half the cookies in bottom of 8 inch (20 cm) square pan.

▼ **PREPARE** pudding mix with 1 cup (250 mL) milk as directed on package. Fold in whipped topping.

▼ **POUR** half the pudding mixture over cookies in pan. Layer remaining cookies and remaining pudding mixture. Top with orange slices.

▼ **THIN** marmalade with water; spoon over oranges. Chill about 3 hours. Cut into squares.

MAKES 9 servings.

TIP: *Use JELL-O Chocolate Instant Pudding instead of Vanilla, if desired.*

Above: Stipe It Rich, Chocolate Wafer-Orange Dessert

QUICK PARFAIT

Prep time: 20 minutes   Chill time: 1 hour

¾ cup	boiling water	175 mL
1 pkg	(10.0 g) JELL-O Light Raspberry Jelly Powder or your favourite flavour	1 pkg
½ cup	cold water	125 mL
	Ice cubes	
½ cup	thawed COOL WHIP or COOL WHIP Light Whipped Topping	125 mL

▼ **POUR** boiling water into blender container. Add jelly powder and blend at low speed until dissolved, about 30 seconds.

▼ **COMBINE** cold water and ice cubes to make 1¼ cups (300 mL). Add to jelly and stir until ice is partially melted, then blend at high speed for 10 seconds. Add whipped topping and blend 15 seconds.

▼ **POUR** mixture into straight-sided parfait glasses.

Chill until set, about 1 hour.

MAKES about 3 cups (750 mL) or 6 servings.

TIP: Scrape down sides of blender to ensure all jelly is dissolved, using a rubber spatula.
PER SERVING:
Calories 26, Protein 1 g, Fat 1.6 g,
Carbohydrate 1.5 g

APPLESTICK SNACK

Prep time: 5 minutes   Chill time: 1 hour

1 pkg	(10.1 g) JELL-O Light Strawberry Jelly Powder	1 pkg
1 cup	boiling water	250 mL
½ cup	apple juice	125 mL
1 cup	ice cubes	250 mL
1	medium unpeeled red, yellow or green apple, cut in sticks	1

▼ **DISSOLVE** jelly powder in boiling water. Add apple juice and ice cubes stirring until jelly is slightly thickened. Remove any unmelted ice. Add apple.

▼ **SPOON** into serving dishes. Chill until set, about 1 hour.

MAKES 4 servings.

TIP: Substitute Bosc or Bartlett pear "sticks" for the apple, if desired.
PER SERVING:
Calories 43, Protein 1.5 g, Fat 0.2 g,
Carbohydrate 9.1 g, Dietary Fibre 0.7 g

Opposite page: Applestick Snack, Quick Parfait, Jelly Sparkle

▼ ▼ ▼

▼ ▼ ▼ ▼ ▼ ▼ ▼

LAYERED FRUIT DESSERT

Prep time: 20 minutes

2 cups	strawberry halves	**500 mL**
2	peaches, peeled, cubed	**2**
1 cup	fresh blueberries	**250 mL**
2 cups	seedless green grapes, halved	**500 mL**
1 pkg	JELL-O Light Instant Vanilla Pudding	**1 pkg**
2 cups	milk (2 %)	**500 mL**
½ cup	yogurt, plain or fruit flavoured	**125 mL**

▼ **LAYER** fruits in medium glass serving bowl or individual parfait dishes.

▼ **PREPARE** pudding as directed on package. Fold in yogurt. Spoon over fruit.

▼ **SERVE** immediately.

MAKES 4 servings, ½ cup (125 mL) each.

> **TIP:** *Substitute 6 cups (1.5 L) unsweetened drained canned fruit for the fresh.*
>
> **PER SERVING:**
> Calories 225,   Protein 7.2 g,   Fat 4.1 g,
> Carbohydrate 43.2 g,   Dietary Fibre 4.4 g

DID YOU KNOW ABOUT YOGURT:

Yogurt is a cultured milk, much like buttermilk, sour cream, and crème fraîche. It develops from the action of bacteria. Calories and nutrients differ from brand to brand, use low fat yogurt for less fat.

▼ ▼ ▼

CHOCOLATE ANGEL DESSERT

Prep time: 15 minutes   Chill time: 15 minutes

1½ cups	small angel food cake cubes	**375 mL**
1 cup	raspberries, sliced strawberries or sliced bananas	**250 mL**
1½ cups	cold milk (2 %)	**375 mL**
1 pkg	(4-serving size) JELL-O Light Chocolate Instant Pudding	**1 pkg**
1 cup	thawed COOL WHIP Light Whipped Topping	**250 mL**

▼ **DIVIDE** cake cubes and fruit evenly among 6 dessert dishes; set aside.

▼ **POUR** milk into medium bowl; add pudding mix. Beat with wire whisk 1 to 2 minutes or until well blended. Let stand 5 minutes.

▼ **GENTLY** fold in whipped topping. Spoon into dessert dishes. Chill 15 minutes.

   MAKES 6 servings.

Quick and Easy Light Jell-O Mousse - Ready in 5 minutes! Prepare instant pudding according to package directions. Stir in 1½ cups (375 mL) thawed COOL WHIP Light Whipped Topping. Spoon into dessert dishes.

PER SERVING:
Calories 109,   Protein 3.3 g,   Fat 3.1 g,
Carbohydrate 18 g,   Dietary Fibre 1.0 g

Above from left to right: Layered Fruit Dessert, Chocolate Angel Dessert

▼ ▼ ▼ ▼ ▼ ▼ ▼
FRUIT TERRINE SUPREME

Prep time: 20 minutes   Chill time: 4 hours

Fruit Terrine

2 pkg	(9.1 g **each**) JELL-O Light Lemon Jelly Powder	2 pkg
1½ cups	boiling water	375 mL
¾ cup	orange juice	175 mL
	Ice cubes	
2 tsp	grated orange rind	10 mL
1 tub	(1 L) thawed COOL WHIP Whipped Topping	1 tub

Blueberry Sauce

1 pkg	(300 g) frozen unsweetened blueberries, thawed	1 pkg
2 Tbsp	lemon juice	25 mL
⅓ cup	sugar or equivalent artificial sweetener	75 mL
2 Tbsp	water	25 mL

FRUIT TERRINE:

▼ **DISSOLVE** jelly powder in boiling water. Combine orange juice and ice cubes to make 1¾ cups (425 mL). Add to jelly, stirring until ice is melted. Stir in orange rind. Chill until slightly thickened.

▼ **FOLD** topping into jelly mixture. Spoon into 9 x 5 inch (23 x 13cm) loaf pan. Chill 4 hours or overnight. To unmould dip in warm water for 15 seconds and invert onto cutting board or serving platter. Slice and serve with Blueberry Sauce.

MAKES 10 servings.

BLUEBERRY SAUCE:

▼ **COMBINE** blueberries, lemon juice, sugar and water in medium saucepan. (If using artificial sweetener add last.) Bring to a boil.

▼ **COOK** and stir over medium heat for 2 to 3 minutes. Process in food processor or blender for 1 minute until smooth. (Add sweetener to taste.) Chill. Stir well before serving. Makes about 1 cup (250 mL).

TIP: Substitute unsweetened frozen or fresh strawberries or raspberries for the blueberries, if desired.

PER SERVING:
Calories 157,   Protein 1.7 g,   Fat 8.3 g,
Carbohydrate 19.9 g,   Dietary Fibre 1.0 g

DID YOU KNOW HOW TO PROTECT YOUR BAKING PANS:

For metal baking pans, wash in hot soapy water, rinse well. Place in a warm (200° F/95° C) oven. Turn off oven and leave ½ hour to dry. This will prevent rusting and will also prevent colour from 'leaching' into food. If your pans are already 'old', line with plastic wrap for non-baked desserts.

▼ ▼ ▼

LIGHT'N FRUITY STRAWBERRY PIE

Prep time: 20 minutes   Chill time: 3 hours

1 pkg	(10.1 g) JELL-O Light Strawberry Jelly Powder	1 pkg
⅔ cup	boiling water	150 mL
2 cups	ice cubes	500 mL
1 tub	(1 L) thawed COOL WHIP Light Whipped Topping	1 tub
1 cup	crushed fresh strawberries	250 mL
1	prepared 9 inch (23 cm) graham wafer crumb crust	1

▼ **DISSOLVE** jelly powder in boiling water. Add ice cubes and stir constantly until jelly starts to thicken, 3 to 5 minutes. Remove any unmelted ice.

▼ **WHISK** in whipped topping gently until smooth. Fold in fruit. Chill until thick, about 15 minutes.

▼ **SPOON** into crust. Chill 3 hours.

MAKES 8 servings.

TIP: *For Raspberry Pie, substitute with JELL-O Light Raspberry Jelly Powder and raspberries for the strawberries.*

PER SERVING:
Calories 198, Protein 2.2 g, Fat 10.1 g, Carbohydrate 26 g, Dietary Fibre 0.9 g

Above: Light'n Fruity Strawberry Pie

LIGHT LEMON CHEESECAKE

Prep time: 15 minutes   Chill time: 4 hours

3 Tbsp	graham wafer crumbs	**45 mL**
1 pkg	(9.1 g) JELL-O Light Lemon Jelly Powder	**1 pkg**
²/₃ cup	boiling water	**150 mL**
2 pkg	(250 g **each**) Light PHILADELPHIA Cream Cheese, cubed	**2 pkg**
	Grated rind of 2 lemons	
	Juice of 1 lemon	
2 cups	thawed COOL WHIP Whipped Topping	**500 mL**

▼ **SPRINKLE** crumbs onto sides of 8 inch (20 cm) springform pan which has been sprayed with nonstick cooking spray.

▼ **PLACE** jelly powder in blender container. Add water; blend on low speed until dissolved. Add cream cheese; blend at medium speed until smooth, scraping sides of blender. Pour into large bowl.

▼ **FOLD** in lemon rind, juice and topping. Pour into prepared pan; smooth top. Chill 4 hours. Serve with fresh fruit.

MAKES 12 servings.

TIP: *For easier squeezing of lemons, have at room temperature and roll lemon on counter lightly before squeezing.*

PER SERVING:
Calories 154, Protein 4.1 g, Fat 12.8 g, Carbohydrate 6 g, Dietary Fibre 0.1 g

Above: Light Lemon Cheesecake

Above: Cherry Waldorf Salad, Fiesta Carrot Pineapple Salad

▼ ▼ ▼ ▼ ▼ ▼ ▼

CHERRY WALDORF SALAD

Prep time: 10 minutes   Chill time: 30 minutes

1 pkg	(11.2 g) JELL-O Light Cherry Jelly Powder	1 pkg
¾ cup	boiling water	175 mL
½ cup	cold water	125 mL
	Ice cubes	
½ cup	unpeeled diced apple	125 mL
1	small banana, sliced	1
¼ cup	sliced celery	50 mL

▼ **DISSOLVE** jelly powder in boiling water. Combine cold water and ice cubes to make 1¼ cups (300 mL). Add to jelly and stir until slightly thickened; remove any unmelted ice.

▼ **FOLD** in fruits and celery. Chill in individual dishes until set, about 30 minutes. Makes about 2½ cups (625 mL) or 5 servings.

TIPS: Substitute 1 orange, peeled and sectioned, for the banana, if desired.
Pour into a 4 cup (1 L) mould and chill 3 hours, if desired. Unmould and serve.

PER SERVING:
Calories 32,   Protein 1.5 g,   Fat 0.1 g,
Carbohydrate 6.4 g,   Dietary Fibre 0.6 g

FIESTA CARROT PINEAPPLE SALAD

Prep time: 2 hours   Chill time: 2 hours or overnight

1 pkg	(9.3 g) JELL-O Light Fruit Feista or (9.1 g) JELL-O Light Lemon Jelly Powder	1 pkg
1 cup	boiling water	250 mL
1 can	(14 oz/398 mL) pineapple tidbits in own juice	1 can
½ cup	shredded carrot	125 mL

▼ **DISSOLVE** jelly powder in boiling water. Drain pineapple tidbits reserving liquid; add cold water to measure 1 cup (250 mL); stir into jelly.

▼ **CHILL** jelly until slightly thickened, about 1¼ hours.

▼ **STIR** in pineapple tidbits and shredded carrots. Pour into 4 cup (1 L) bowl. Chill until set.

MAKES 6 servings.

TIP: Pour jelly mixture into lightly greased muffin cups, chill and unmould for individual servings.

PER SERVING:
Calories 51,   Protein 1.3 g,   Fat 0.1 g,
Carbohydrate 12 g,   Dietary Fibre 0.8 g

▼ ▼ ▼

Above: Very Berry, Sunshine Squeeze

VERY BERRY

Prep time: 15 minutes   Chill time: 30 minutes

1 pkg	(10.1 g) JELL-O Light Strawberry Jelly Powder	1 pkg
1 cup	thawed COOL WHIP Whipped Topping	250 mL
1 cup	fresh sliced strawberries	250 mL

▼ **PREPARE** jelly powder according to 30 Minute Set Method on package. Measure ½ cup (125 mL) of jelly. Whisk into topping. Spoon into dessert dishes. Chill 20 minutes.

▼ **MEANWHILE,** fold strawberries into remaining jelly. Spoon over bottom layer. Chill until set, about 30 minutes.

MAKES 4 servings.

> **TIP:** *To prepare slanted dessert, lean empty parfait glasses against the rim of a square pan. Secure with tape and support underneath with folded paper towel. Prepare creamy layer as above and spoon into glasses. Chill as above. Stand upright and spoon fruited jelly over bottom layer. Chill until set.*
>
> **PER SERVING:**
> Calories 79, Protein 1.8 g, Fat 4.9 g, Carbohydrate 7.1 g, Dietary Fibre 0.8 g

---

SUNSHINE SQUEEZE

Prep time: 15 minutes   Chill time: 30 minutes

1 pkg	(10.2 g) JELL-O Light Orange Jelly Powder	1 pkg
1 cup	orange sections	250 mL

▼ **PREPARE** jelly powder according to 30 Minute Set Method on package.

▼ **SET ASIDE** ½ cup (125 mL). Chill until slightly thickened.

▼ **FOLD** orange sections into remaining jelly. Spoon into 6 dessert dishes.

▼ **BEAT** reserved jelly with mixer until double in volume. Spoon over fruited layer. Chill until set, about 30 minutes.

MAKES 4 servings.

> **TIP:** *For best volume when beating jelly, place in a small bowl and beat at high speed with an electric mixer.*
>
> **PER SERVING:**
> Calories 29, Protein 1.8 g, Fat 0.1 g, Carbohydrate 5.4 g, Dietary Fibre 0.8 g

---

DID YOU KNOW ABOUT ORANGES:

Low in calories and sodium and high in vitamin C. Oranges come in many varieties from Blood oranges to Temple oranges. They should be firm and heavy for their size when purchased, smooth and unblemished. Store at room temperature for 3 to 4 days or in plastic bags in the refridgerator.

Above: Amazing Melon Wedge, Light Fruit Treasure Cup

▼▼▼▼▼▼

AMAZING MELON WEDGE

Prep time: 10 minutes   Chill time: 3 hours

1	medium melon	1
1 pkg	(10.3 g) JELL-O Light Lime Jelly Powder	1 pkg

▼ **CUT** melon in half lengthwise; scoop out seeds; drain well. Dry inside with paper towel.

▼ **PREPARE** jelly powder according to 30 Minute Set Method on package.

▼ **PLACE** melon halves in small bowls and spoon jelly into centres. Chill until firm, about 3 hours. To serve, cut in wedges or slices.

MAKES 6 servings.

TIP: Use any flavour of JELL-O. Use cantaloupe or honeydew, if desired.
PER SERVING:
Calories 81, Protein 1.9 g, Fat 0.2 g, Carbohydrate 19.7 g, Dietary Fibre 1.7 g

LIGHT FRUIT TREASURE CUP

Prep time: 5 minutes   Chill time: 30 minutes

1 pkg	(10.1 g) JELL-O Light Strawberry Jelly Powder	1 pkg
1 can	(14 oz/398 mL) fruit cocktail, drained	1 can
1 cup	low fat cottage cheese	250 mL

▼ **PREPARE** jelly powder according to 30 Minute Set Method on package.

▼ **STIR** fruit cocktail into slightly thickened jelly.

▼ **DIVIDE** cottage cheese among 4 dessert dishes. Top with fruit jelly mixture. Chill until set, about 30 minutes.

MAKES 4 servings.

TIP: Substitute plain yogurt for the cottage cheese, if desired.
PER SERVING:
Calories 87, Protein 9.5 g, Fat 0.6 g, Carbohydrate 10.3 g, Dietary Fibre 0.8 g

---

DID YOU KNOW ABOUT PREVENTING FRUIT FROM BROWNING:

Fruits such as sliced apples, pears, peaches, and bananas will brown when exposed to the air. Sprinkle with orange, lemon or lime juice to prevent browning.

▼▼▼

Above: Fruited Squares, Foamy Peach Snack

▼▼▼▼▼▼

FRUITED SQUARES

Prep time: 10 minutes   Chill time: 3 hours

2 pkg	(10.1 g **each**) JELL-O Light Strawberry Jelly Powder or your favourite flavour	2 pkg
1½ cups	boiling water	375 mL
1 cup	cold water	250 mL
2 cups	thawed COOL WHIP or COOL WHIP Light Whipped Topping	500 mL
1 can	(14 oz/398 mL) fruit cocktail in fruit juice or light syrup, drained*	1 can

* or use 1 cup (250 mL) sliced fresh fruit.

▼ **DISSOLVE** jelly powder in boiling water. Combine cold water and ice cubes to make 2 cups (500 mL). Add to jelly and stir until slightly thickened; remove any unmelted ice. Measure 1 cup (250 mL) and fold into whipped topping; pour into 8 inch (20 cm) square pan.

▼ **ARRANGE** fruit on creamy layer, then spoon remaining jelly over fruit. Chill until firm, about 3 hours. Cut into 9 squares.

MAKES 9, ½ cup (125 mL) servings.

> *TIP: Variations - Raspberry or strawberry jelly powder with sliced pineapple or peaches.*
> *- Cherry or lime jelly powder with sliced banana or pears.*
> *- Orange jelly powder with apricot halves.*
> **PER SERVING (1 square):**
> Calories 75, Protein 1.6 g, Fat 4.2 g,
> Carbohydrate 7.7 g, Dietary Fibre 0.3 g

FOAMY PEACH SNACK

Prep time: 10 minutes   Chill time: 1 hour

1 can	(14 oz/398 mL) sliced peaches, in fruit juice	1 can
1 pkg	(10.0 g) JELL-O Light Raspberry Jelly Powder	1 pkg
½ cup	ice cubes	125 mL

▼ **DRAIN** peaches, reserving juice. Add water to juice to make ¾ cup (175 mL); bring measured liquid to a boil.

▼ **POUR** boiling liquid into blender container. Add jelly powder and blend at low speed until dissolved, about 1 minute.

▼ **ADD** ice cubes and blend at low speed until ice is partially melted. Add peaches and blend at high speed until ice is melted, about 30 seconds.

▼ **POUR** into 6 dessert dishes. Chill until set, about 1 hour.

MAKES 6 servings.

> *TIP: Substitute 1 cup (250 mL) fresh raspberries for the peaches, if desired.*
> **PER SERVING:**
> Calories 36, Protein 1.4 g, Fat 0 g,
> Carbohydrate 8.1 g, Dietary Fibre 0.7 g

▼▼▼

▼▼ ▼▼▼▼ ▼▼

STRAWBERRY YOGURT FLUFF

Prep time: 5 minutes   Chill time: 1 hour

¾ cup	boiling water	**175 mL**
1 pkg	(10.1 g) JELL-O Light Strawberry Jelly Powder	**1 pkg**
½ cup	cold water	**125 mL**
	Ice cubes	
1 cup	plain, low fat yogurt	**250 mL**
	Fresh strawberries for garnish (optional)	

▼ **POUR** boiling water into blender container. Add jelly powder and blend at low speed until dissolved, about 1 minute.

▼ **COMBINE** cold water and ice cubes to make 1 cup (250 mL). Add to jelly and stir until ice is almost melted. Remove unmelted ice. Blend in yogurt.

▼ **CHILL** in dessert dishes until set, about 1 hour. If desired, garnish with fresh strawberries.

MAKES 4 servings.

TIP: For best results when dissolving jelly powder in blender, scrape sides with rubber spatula after 1 minute.

PER SERVING:
Calories 39,   Protein 3.5 g,   Fat 1.2 g, Carbohydrate 3 g

Above: Strawberry Yogurt Fluff

▼ ▼ ▼

TRADITIONAL FRUIT TRIFLE

Prep time: 30 minutes   Chill time: 2 hours or overnight

Jelly layer

4 cups	pound cake cubes	1 L
2 Tbsp	sweet sherry	25 mL
1 can	(14 oz/398 mL) fruit cocktail, drained	1 can
1 pkg	(85 g) JELL-O Strawberry Jelly Powder	1 pkg

Custard layer

1 pkg	(4-serving size) JELL-O Vanilla Pudding and Pie Filling	1 pkg
2 Tbsp	sweet sherry	25 mL
2 cups	thawed COOL WHIP Whipped Topping	500 mL

JELLY LAYER:

▼ **PLACE** cake cubes in large 10 cup (2.5 L) serving bowl; sprinkle with sherry. Add fruit cocktail.

▼ **PREPARE** jelly powder according to 30 Minute Set Method on package. Spoon slightly thickened jelly over fruit cocktail; chill until set.

CUSTARD LAYER:

▼ **PREPARE** pudding and pie filling mix as directed on package increasing milk to 2½ cups (625 mL). Add sherry. Cover with plastic wrap; chill.

Measure ⅔ cup (150 mL) whipped topping; set aside.

▼ **FOLD** pudding into remaining whipped topping. Spoon over jelly in bowl. Chill at least 2 hours.

▼ **GARNISH** with reserved whipped topping. If desired, garnish with nuts and candied cherries.

MAKES 8 to 10 servings.

TIP: Trifle may be made up to 2 days ahead. If desired, substitute 2 cups (500 mL) chopped fresh fruit for the fruit cocktail.

DID YOU KNOW ABOUT MAKING BAKER'S CHOCOLATE CURLS:

Warm the chocolate slightly until the texture is pliable enough to curl. Chocolate can be warmed by holding the wrapped square in the palm of your hand until chocolate softens slightly, or microwave on DEFROST for approximately 1 minute per square. When the chocolate is slightly softened and pliable, carefully draw a vegatable peeler over the smooth surface of the square. Use a toothpick to gently lift the curls without breaking them.

CHERRY TOPPED EGGNOG RING

Prep time: 1 hour   Chill time: 4 hours or overnight

1 can	(284 mL) mandarin orange segments	1 can
1 pkg	(85 g) JELL-O Cherry or Cranberry Jelly Powder	1 pkg
1 cup	boiling water	250 mL
1 cup	chopped apple	250 mL
1 pkg	(85 g) JELL-O Lemon Jelly Powder	1 pkg
1 cup	boiling water	250 mL
¾ cup	canned or dairy eggnog	175 mL
¼ cup	cold water	50 mL
1 tsp	dark rum (optional)	5 mL
2 cups	thawed COOL WHIP Whipped Topping	500 mL

▼ **DRAIN** mandarin oranges, measuring syrup. Add water to syrup to make 1 cup (250 mL).

▼ **DISSOLVE** cherry jelly powder in 1 cup (250 mL) boiling water. Add measured liquid. Chill until slightly thickened, about 1¼ hours. Add mandarin oranges and apples.

▼ **SPOON** into a large 6 cup (1.5 L) jelly mould. Chill.

▼ **MEANWHILE,** dissolve lemon jelly powder in 1 cup (250 mL) boiling water. Cool to room temperature Add eggnog, cold water and rum. Chill until slightly thickened, about 1¼ hours.

▼ **FOLD** eggnog mixture into 1 cup (250 mL) whipped topping. Spoon over fruit jelly layer in mould.

▼ **CHILL** until set, about 4 hours or overnight. Unmould onto chilled serving plate. Garnish with remaining topping.

MAKES 10 servings.

> **TIP:** *Garnish with sugar coated cherries, if desired. To sugar coat, beat 1 egg white until frothy. Dip cherries in the egg white and then in granulated sugar.*

Opposite page: Traditional Fruit Trifle   ▼▼▼   *Above: Cherry Topped Eggnog Ring*

▼ ▼ ▼ ▼ ▼ ▼

Above: Gingerbread People,
Microwave Popcorn Balls

▼ ▼ ▼

▼▼▼▼▼▼

GINGERBREAD PEOPLE

Prep time: 20 minutes   Baking time: 10 to 12 minutes

1 pkg	(6-serving size) JELL-O Butterscotch Pudding and Pie Filling	**1 pkg**
¾ cup	butter	**175 mL**
¾ cup	firmly packed brown sugar	**175 mL**
1	egg	**1**
2¼ cups	all-purpose flour	**550 mL**
1 tsp	baking soda	**5 mL**
1 Tbsp	ground ginger	**15 mL**
1½ tsp	ground cinnamon	**7 mL**

▼ **CREAM** pudding and pie filling mix with butter and sugar. Add egg and blend well.

▼ **COMBINE** flour, baking soda, ginger and cinnamon; blend into pudding mixture. Chill dough until firm, about 1 hour.

▼ **ROLL** on a floured board to about ¼ inch (0.5 cm) thickness and cut with cookie cutter.

▼ **PLACE** on greased baking sheets; use a straw to make a hole in the top of the cookie for hanging on the tree.

▼ **BAKE** at 350°F (180°C) for 10 to 12 minutes. Remove from oven and cool on wire rack. Decorate as desired.

MAKES 16 to 18 gingerbread cookies.

TIP: Small icing tubes are ideal for decorating cookies.

MICROWAVE POPCORN BALLS

Prep time:10 minutes

¼ cup	butter	**50 mL**
6 cups	miniature marshmallows	**1500 mL**
1 pkg	(85 g) JELL-O Jelly Powder, any flavour	**1 pkg**
12 cups	popped popcorn	**3 L**
1 cup	peanuts (optional)	**250 mL**

▼ **PLACE** butter and marshmallows in large microwavable bowl. Cook in microwave on HIGH power for 1½ to 2 minutes or until marshmallows are puffed.

▼ **ADD** dry jelly powder; stir until well blended.

▼ **POUR** marshmallow mixture over combined popcorn and peanuts. Stir quickly to coat well.

▼ **SHAPE** into balls, teddy bears or other shapes with greased hands. Decorate as desired.

MAKES about 36 popcorn balls.

TIP: Substitute raisins for the peanuts, if desired. Work quickly when combining marshmallow mixture and popcorn as mixture will thicken.

▼▼▼

▼ ▼ ▼ ▼ ▼ ▼

FAMILY FAVOURITE NANAIMO BARS

Prep time: 30 minutes   Chill time: 3 hours

3 squares	BAKER'S Unsweetened Chocolate	3 sq
½ cup	butter	125 mL
1½ cups	graham wafer crumbs	375 mL
½ cup	finely chopped toasted pecans	125 mL
1 pkg	(4-serving size) JELL-O Vanilla Instant Pudding	1 pkg
⅓ cup	**each:** butter and boiling water	75 mL
2 cups	icing sugar	500 mL
3 squares	BAKER'S Semi-Sweet Chocolate	3 sq
½ cup	whipping cream	125 mL

▼ **MELT** unsweetened chocolate and ½ cup (125 mL) butter over low heat; remove. Add crumbs and pecans; mix well.

▼ **PRESS** into 9 inch (23 cm) square pan. Chill.

▼ **COMBINE** pudding mix, ⅓ cup (75 mL) butter and water; blend in icing sugar until smooth. Spread over crust; chill until set, about 1 hour.

▼ **MELT** semi-sweet chocolate and cream over low heat; stir until smooth. Spread over pudding layer. Chill.

▼ **STORE** in refrigerator; let stand at room temperature 30 minutes before slicing. Sprinkle with icing sugar, if desired.

MAKES 24 bars.

TIP: Use any flavour of pudding, as desired. Store in an airtight container in refrigerator up to 1 week.

CAPPUCCINO CUPS

Prep time: 15 minutes   Freeze time: 6 hours

12	chocolate wafers	12
2 Tbsp	instant coffee granules	25 mL
¼ cup	hot water	50 mL
1½ cups	half and half cream or milk	375 mL
1 pkg	(4-serving size) JELL-O Vanilla Instant Pudding	1 pkg
¼ tsp	ground cinnamon	1 mL
3½ cups	thawed COOL WHIP Whipped Topping	875 mL
2 squares	Baker's Semi-Sweet Chocolate, melted	2 sq

▼ **PLACE** 1 cookie in bottom of 12 paper-lined muffin cups.

▼ **DISSOLVE** instant coffee in hot water in medium bowl. Add cream, pudding mix and cinnamon. Beat with whisk about 2 minutes. Let stand 5 minutes or until slightly thickened.

▼ **FOLD** in whipped topping. Spoon into muffin cups. Freeze until firm, about 6 hours.

▼ **REMOVE** dessert from paper cup. Place on individual dessert plate. Drizzle melted chocolate over each dessert cup.

MAKES 12 individual cups.

TIP: Garnish with chocolate covered coffee beans, if desired.

▼ ▼ ▼

▼ ▼ ▼ ▼ ▼ ▼

EASY GRASSHOPPER PIE

Prep time: 20 minutes   Chill time: 3 hours or overnight

1 pkg	(85 g) JELL-O Lime Jelly Powder	**1 pkg**
²/₃ cup	boiling water	**150 mL**
2 cups	ice cubes	**500 mL**
1 cup	thawed COOL WHIP Whipped Topping	**250 mL**
2 Tbsp	Creme de Menthe liqueur	**25 mL**
1	prepared 9 inch (23 cm) graham wafer crumb crust	**1**

▼ **DISSOLVE** jelly powder in boiling water. Add ice cubes and stir constantly until jelly starts to thicken, about 3 to 5 minutes. Remove any unmelted ice.

▼ **ADD** whipped topping and liqueur to jelly and whisk until well blended.

▼ **SPOON** into crumb crust. Chill 3 hours. Garnish with lime slices or mint leaves, if desired.

MAKES 8 servings.

TIP: If you don't have Creme de Menthe, substitute 1 tsp (5 mL) mint extract and several drops green food colouring.

CHERRY REVEL

Prep time: 30 minutes   Chill time: 4 hours or overnight

3 squares	BAKER'S Semi-Sweet Chocolate, chopped	**3 sq**
2 pkg	(85 g **each**) JELL-O Cherry Jelly Powder	**2 pkg**
2 cups	boiling water	**500 mL**
4 cups	ice cubes	**1 L**
1 tub	(1 L) thawed COOL WHIP Whipped Topping	**1 tub**
1 cup	cherry pie filling	**250 mL**
3 squares	BAKER'S Semi-Sweet Chocolate (for garnish)	**3 sq**

Maraschino cherries with stems

▼ **MELT** chocolate in microwavable bowl on MEDIUM power about 2 minutes. Stir until smooth. Drizzle chocolate on inside of 8 to 10 cup (2 to 2.5 L) glass bowl using a spoon. Refrigerate bowl.

▼ **DISSOLVE** jelly powder in boiling water. Add ice and stir until jelly begins to thicken. Remove any unmelted ice. Whisk in 3 cups (750 mL) whipped topping and chill until mixture is slightly thickened, about 20 minutes. Fold in cherry pie filling and spoon into glass bowl. Chill 4 hours or overnight.

▼ **JUST** before serving, garnish top with remaining topping, chocolate curls and cherries.

MAKES 10 to 12 servings.

TIP: Cool chocolate slightly to prevent running down sides of bowl.

▼ ▼ ▼

TRUFFLE TREATS

Prep time: 15 minutes   Freeze time: 4 hours or overnight

6 squares	BAKER'S Semi-Sweet Chocolate	**6 sq**
¼ cup	butter	**50 mL**
1 pkg	(200 g) BAKER'S ANGEL FLAKE Coconut	**1 pkg**
1 pkg	(250 g) PHILADELPHIA Cream Cheese, softened	**1 pkg**
2½ cups	milk or half and half cream	**625 mL**
1 pkg	(4-serving size) JELL-O Instant Chocolate Pudding	**1 pkg**
1 cup	thawed COOL WHIP Whipped Topping	**250 mL**
2 squares	BAKER'S Semi-Sweet Chocolate, grated	**2 sq**

▼ **LINE** a 13 x 9 inch (33 x 23 cm) baking pan with waxed paper to extend over the sides of the pan.

▼ **HEAT** chocolate and butter over low heat or in microwave on MEDIUM power for 2 minutes, until butter is melted. Stir until completely smooth; reserve 2 Tbsp (25 mL).

▼ **STIR** chocolate into coconut; toss to coat evenly. Press mixture into baking pan.

▼ **BEAT** cream cheese at medium speed of electric mixer until smooth; beat in reserved chocolate. Gradually beat in milk.

▼ **ADD** pudding mix. Beat at low speed until well blended, about 2 minutes. Gently fold in

whipped topping. Pour over crust. Sprinkle with grated chocolate, pressing lightly. Freeze until firm, about 4 hours or overnight.

▼ **REMOVE** from freezer. Run knife around outside. Lift from pan onto cutting board. Removed waxed paper. Cut into diamonds, squares or triangles. Store leftover treats in the refrigerator or freezer.

MAKES about 20 treats.

TIP: Sprinkle squares with icing sugar, if desired.

DID YOU KNOW ABOUT PHILADELPHIA CREAM CHEESE:

Cream cheese originated in Chester, New York in 1872 and is made from a combination of milk and cream which gives it a special smooth richness. Cream cheese is a fresh cheese which is moist, unripened, and unfermented. Philadelphia Cream Cheese produced by Kraft is one of the best known of all cream cheeses. Cream cheese can be plain or spiced or seasoned. It is best used as spreads, dips, sauces or in desserts such as cheesecakes.

Opposite page: Easy Tiramisu, Truffle Treats

▼ ▼ ▼ ▼ ▼ ▼

EASY TIRAMISU

Prep time: 30 minutes   Cook time: 10 minutes   Chill time: 4 hours

1 pkg	(6-serving size) JELL-O Vanilla Pudding and Pie Filling	**1 pkg**
1 pkg	(250 g) PHILADELPHIA Cream Cheese, softened	**1 pkg**
¼ cup	coffee liqueur	**50 mL**
1 Tbsp	instant coffee granules	**15 mL**
½ cup	hot water	**125 mL**
1 Tbsp	granulated sugar	**15 mL**
1 pkg	(7 oz/200 g) lady fingers	**1 pkg**
1½ cups	thawed COOL WHIP Whipped Topping	**375 mL**
4 squares	BAKER'S Semi-Sweet Chocolate, coarsely grated	**4 sq**

▼ **PREPARE** pudding and pie filling mix according to package directions. Beat cream cheese and coffee liqueur into hot filling. Cover with plastic wrap and chill 1 hour.

▼ **COMBINE** coffee, hot water and sugar; brush over lady fingers.

▼ **FOLD** whipped topping into pudding mixture.

▼ **LINE** bottom of 8 cup (2 L) trifle bowl with ½ of the lady fingers. Spread ½ of pudding mixture over lady fingers; sprinkle with ½ of the grated chocolate. Repeat layers. Cover tightly; chill 4 hours or overnight to blend flavours.

MAKES 10 to 12 servings.

DID YOU KNOW ABOUT GRATING BAKER'S CHOCOLATE:

Use a fine or coarse grater. For larger pieces, use a coarse grater and warm the chocolate as you would for chocolate curls. Grate chocolate onto a piece of waxed paper. A food processor with a grating disc works well too.

▼ ▼ ▼

LEMON CHEESE PIE

Prep time: 25 minutes   Chill time: 3 hours

1	baked 9 inch (23 cm) pastry crust	1
1 pkg	(113 g) JELL-O Lemon Pie Filling	1 pkg
½ cup	granulated sugar	125 mL
1¼ cups	water	300 mL
2	egg yolks	2
1 cup	milk	250 mL
1 pkg	(125 g) PHILADELPHIA Cream Cheese, softened	1 pkg
1 Tbsp	butter	15 mL
2	egg whites	2
¼ cup	granulated sugar	50 mL

▼ **CHILL** baked crust.

▼ **COMBINE** pie filling mix, ½ cup (125 mL) sugar and ¼ cup (50 mL) of the water in saucepan. Blend in egg yolks, remaining 1 cup (250 mL) water and milk.

▼ **COOK,** stirring constantly, over medium heat until mixture comes to a full bubbling boil.

▼ **BEAT** cream cheese in a small bowl until smooth. Beat ½ of pie filling into cheese. Stir butter into remaining ½ of pie filling.

▼ **BEAT** egg whites until foamy throughout. Gradually beat in ¼ cup (50 mL) sugar and con-

tinue beating until mixture forms stiff shiny peaks.

▼ **FOLD** egg whites into lemon-cheese mixture. Spread evenly in baked pie crust. Chill 5 minutes.

▼ **SPOON** remaining pie filling evenly over filling in pie crust. Chill 3 hours before serving.

MAKES about 8 servings.

> *TIP: For extra lemon flavour, substitute 2 Tbsp (25 mL) lemon juice for 2 Tbsp (25) water and add 1 tsp (5 mL) grated lemon rind to pudding.*

LEMON COCONUT BARS

Prep time: 20 minutes   Baking time: 50 to 60 minutes

½ cup	butter	125 mL
¼ cup	icing sugar	50 mL
1¼ cups	all-purpose flour	300 mL
2	eggs	2
½ cup	granulated sugar	125 mL
1	pkg (113 g) JELL-O Lemon Pie Filling	1 pkg
½ tsp	baking powder	2 mL
1 cup	chopped dates	250 mL
1½ cups	BAKER'S ANGEL FLAKE Coconut	375 mL
	Icing sugar	

▼ **CREAM** butter and icing sugar. Add flour and mix well.

▼ **PRESS** evenly into bottom of 8 inch (20 cm) square pan.

▼ **BAKE** at 350°F (180°C) for 20 to 25 minutes, until lightly browned.

▼ **MEANWHILE,** beat eggs until thick and light in colour. Gradually beat in granulated sugar.

▼ **BLEND** in pie filling mix and baking powder. Fold in dates and coconut.

▼ **SPREAD** over hot baked crust. Return to oven and bake 30 to 35 minutes longer, until golden brown. Cool.

▼ **SPRINKLE** with icing sugar if desired; cut into bars. Store in tightly covered container.

MAKES 1 to 1½ dozen bars.

TIP: Substitute dried apricots for the dates, if desired.

DID YOU KNOW ABOUT DATES:

To cut dates easily, dip the knife or kitchen scissors in hot water occasionally to prevent sticking. Store in an airtight container in the refrigerator for freshness.

Opposite page: Lemon Coconut Bars, Lemon Cheese Pie

Above: Sparkling Fruits in Strawberry-Kiwi Jelly, shown with vanilla pudding

▼ ▼ ▼ ▼ ▼ ▼ ▼

SPARKLING FRUITS IN STRAWBERRY-KIWI JELLY

Prep time: 40 minutes   Chill time: 3 hours or overnight

Crust

1½ cups	graham wafer crumbs	375 mL
⅓ cup	butter, melted	75 mL
¼ cup	granulated sugar	50 mL

Bottom Layer

2 pkg	(85 g **each**) JELL-O Strawberry-Kiwi or Lemon Jelly Powder	2 pkg
2 cups	boiling water	500 mL
3 cups	vanilla ice cream	750 mL

Top Layer

	Sliced strawberries and lime rind slices for stems	
2 pkg	(85 g **each**) JELL-O Strawberry-Kiwi or Lemon Jelly Powder	2 pkg
1 cup	boiling water	250 mL
1 cup	cold water	250 mL

CRUST:

▼ **COMBINE** crumbs, butter and sugar; press onto base of a 9 inch (23 cm) springform pan. Chill.

BOTTOM LAYER:

▼ **DISSOLVE** jelly powders in boiling water. Whisk spoonfuls of ice cream into jelly until smooth. Chill 15 minutes. Whisk again until smooth. Pour into prepared pan. Chill 45 minutes.

TOP LAYER:

▼ **DECORATIVELY** arrange fruit on bottom layer which should be set but still sticky. Chill while preparing clear layer.

▼ **DISSOLVE** jelly powders in boiling water. Stir in cold water. Chill 15 minutes. Gently spoon a thin layer of jelly over fruit. Chill pan 10 minutes. Spoon on remainder of jelly. Chill 3 hours.

MAKES 10 to 12 servings.

> *TIP: Substitute 30 Minute-Set Method for **TOP LAYER**, if desired. Dissolve jelly powders in 1⅓ cups (300 mL) boiling water. Add 2 cups (500 mL) ice cubes and stir until jelly is slightly thickened. Remove unmelted ice. Stir in 1 cup (250 mL) sliced strawberries. Spoon over ice cream layer. Chill 3 hours or overnight.*

Front cover photo

▼ ▼ ▼

Above: Fluffy Cranberry Orange Pie,
Creamy Lemon Cups

▼ ▼ ▼ ▼ ▼ ▼

CREAMY LEMON CUPS

Prep time: 15 minutes   Chill time: 4 hours or overnight

2 pkg	(85 g **each**) JELL-O Lemon Jelly Powder	**2 pkg**
2 cups	boiling water	**500 mL**
½ **cup**	cold water	**125 mL**
1½ **cups**	cold milk	**375 mL**
1 pkg	(4-serving size) JELL-O Vanilla Instant Pudding	**1 pkg**
½ **tsp**	ground nutmeg	**2 mL**
2 cups	thawed COOL WHIP Whipped Topping	**500 mL**

▼ **DISSOLVE** jelly powder in boiling water. Stir in cold water. Cool to room temperature.

▼ **POUR** milk into another bowl. Add pudding mix. Beat with wire whisk 30 seconds. Immediately stir into cooled jelly until smooth. Stir in nutmeg. Refrigerate about 1½ hours or until slightly thickened.

▼ **STIR** in whipped topping with wire whisk until smooth and creamy. Pour into 10 individual dessert dishes or drinking mugs.

▼ **REFRIGERATE** 4 hours or until firm. Garnish with additional whipped topping and sprinkle with additional ground nutmeg just before serving.

MAKES 10 servings.

TIP: Cut top from lemons. Remove fruit from each. Scrape shells clean with a metal spoon. Fill with lemon mixture. Chill.

FLUFFY CRANBERRY ORANGE PIE

Prep time: 30 minutes   Chill time: 3 hours or overnight

1 pkg	(85 g) JELL-O Cranberry Jelly Powder	**1 pkg**
1 cup	boiling water	**250 mL**
2 cups	ice cubes	**500 mL**
3 cups	thawed COOL WHIP Whipped Topping	**750 mL**
¾ **cup**	whole cranberry sauce	**175 mL**
1 tsp	grated orange rind	**5 mL**
1	prepared 9 inch (23 cm) graham wafer crumb crust	**1**
	Sugared cranberries - optional	

Orange slices, cut into small wedges

▼ **DISSOLVE** jelly powder in boiling water, stirring until completely dissolved, about 2 minutes. Add ice cubes. Stir until jelly thickens about 3 to 5 minutes. Remove any unmelted ice.

▼ **FOLD** jelly into 2½ cups (625 mL) whipped topping; blend until smooth. Fold in cranberry sauce and orange rind.

▼ **REFRIGERATE** 20 minutes or until mixture is thick.

▼ **SPOON** into crumb crust. Refrigerate 3 hours.

▼ **GARNISH** with remaining whipped topping, sugared cranberries and orange slices.

MAKES 8 servings.

TIP: Dip fresh cranberries into lightly beaten egg white; roll in sugar in flat plate to coat well. Place on tray covered with waxed paper.

TRIPLE CHOCOLATE ALMOND PUDDING CAKE

Prep time: 20 minutes   Baking time: 55 to 60 minutes

Cake

1 pkg	(2-layer size) Devil's Food or chocolate cake mix	**1 pkg**
1 pkg	(4-serving size) JELL-O Chocolate Instant Pudding	**1 pkg**
1 cup	sour cream or plain yogurt	**250 mL**
½ cup	vegetable oil	**125 mL**
½ cup	water	**125 mL**
½ cup	toasted chopped almonds	**125 mL**
4	eggs	**4**
3 Tbsp	almond liqueur or 1 tsp (5 mL) almond extract	**45 mL**
1 cup	BAKER'S Semi-Sweet Chocolate Chips	**250 mL**

Glaze

4 squares	BAKER'S Semi-Sweet Chocolate	**4 sq**
2 Tbsp	butter	**25 mL**
2 Tbsp	almond liqueur	**25 mL**
½ tsp	vegetable oil	**2 mL**

CAKE:

▼ **PLACE** all ingredients, except chocolate chips in large mixer bowl and beat for 4 minutes at medium speed. Stir in chocolate chips. Pour into 10 inch (25 cm) greased and floured tube or fluted tube pan.

▼ **BAKE** at 350°F (180°C) for 55 to 60 minutes or until cake springs back when lightly pressed. Let cool in pan for 15 minutes. Remove from pan and leave on rack until completely cooled.

GLAZE:

▼ **MELT** chocolate with butter over hot water. Stir in liqueur and oil. Spoon over cake. Garnish with toasted slivered almonds and chocolate curls, if desired.

MAKES 10 to 12 servings.

> *TIP: Instead of flour, use cocoa powder to dust pan for a darker colour to cake. Substitute a 13 x 9 inch (33 x 23 cm) cake pan, if desired. Adjust baking time.*

Opposite page: Triple Chocolate Almond Pudding Cake

Above: Merry-Go-Round Cake

▼ ▼ ▼ ▼ ▼ ▼

MERRY-GO-ROUND CAKE

Prep time: 30 minutes   Baking time: 50 minutes

1 pkg	(6-serving size) JELL-O Vanilla Instant Pudding	1 pkg
1 pkg	(2-layer size) yellow cake mix	1 pkg
4	eggs	4
1 cup	water	250 mL
¼ cup	vegetable oil	50 mL
⅔ cup	cold milk	150 mL
	Sprinkles (optional)	
	Coloured paper and plastic straws	
	Animal crackers	

▼ **RESERVE** ⅓ cup (75 mL) pudding mix.

▼ **COMBINE** cake mix, remaining pudding mix, eggs, water and oil in large bowl. Beat at low speed of electric mixer just to moisten, scraping sides of bowl often. Beat at medium speed 4 minutes.

▼ **POUR** batter into greased and floured 10 inch (25 cm) fluted tube pan.

▼ **BAKE** at 350°F (180°C) for 50 minutes or until cake tester inserted in centre comes out clean. Cool in pan 15 minutes. Remove from pan; finish cooling on rack.

▼ **BEAT** reserved pudding mix and milk in a small bowl until smooth. Spoon over top of cake to glaze. Garnish with sprinkles, if desired.

▼ **CUT** 10 to 12 inch (25 to 30 cm) circle from coloured paper; scallop edges, if desired. Make 1 slit to centre. Overlap cut edges together to form carousel roof; secure with tape. Cut straws in half; insert around top of cake. Arrange animal crackers at base of straws. Top with roof.

MAKES 12 servings.

> **TIP:** *Use JELL-O Chocolate Instant Pudding and a chocolate cake mix, if desired.*

MELON ANGEL MOUSSE

Prep time: 20 minutes   Chill time: 4 hours or overnight

2 pkg	(85 g **each**) JELL-O Strawberry-Kiwi or Wiggly Watermelon Jelly Powder	2 pkg
2 cups	**each** boiling water and ice cubes	500 mL
1 tub	(1 L) thawed COOL WHIP Whipped Topping	1 tub
1	(200 g) Angel Food cake, cut in small cubes	1
1 cup	**each** cubed canteloupe and honeydew melon	250 mL

▼ **DISSOLVE** jelly powder in boiling water. Add ice cubes, stirring until jelly thickens, about 3 to 5 minutes.

▼ **FOLD** in half of topping; add cake and melon.

▼ **POUR** into 6 cup (1.5 L) bowl lined with plastic wrap.

▼ **CHILL** 4 hours or overnight.

▼ **UNMOULD** onto serving plate; remove plastic. Frost with remaining whipped topping; garnish with additional melon, if desired.

MAKES 10 to 12 servings.

> **TIP:** *Dessert can be made 2 days in advance of serving.*

▼ ▼ ▼ ▼ ▼ ▼

CANADA DAY CELEBRATION SQUARES

Prep time: 30 minutes   Chill time: 30 minutes

1 cup	graham wafer crumbs	**250 mL**
¼ cup	melted butter	**50 mL**
1 pkg	(250 g) PHILADELPHIA Cream Cheese, softened	**1 pkg**
¼ cup	granulated sugar	**50 mL**
1 tub	(1 L) thawed COOL WHIP Whipped Topping	**1 tub**
2 pkg	(85 g **each**) JELL-O Cherry or Strawberry Jelly Powder	**2 pkg**
1 can	(14 oz/398 mL) crushed pineapple, drained	**1 can**
1 square	BAKER'S Semi-Sweet Chocolate, melted	**1 sq**

▼ **MIX** together crumbs and butter. Press firmly in bottom of 13 x 9 inch (33 x 23 cm) baking pan. Refrigerate.

▼ **BEAT** cream cheese and sugar until smooth. Gently fold in half of the topping. Spread over crust.

▼ **PREPARE** jelly powder according to 30 Minute Set Method on package.

▼ **IMMEDIATELY** stir drained fruit into jelly. Spoon over cream cheese layer.

▼ **REFRIGERATE** 30 minutes. Spread remaining topping over jelly.

▼ **DECORATE** with "maple leaf" jigglers, if desired - see Jiggler recipe, page 23.

MAKES 20 pieces.

TIP: Soften cream cheese on DEFROST setting in the microwave for 2 minutes.

DID YOU KNOW ABOUT STAR FRUIT:

Also called carambola, this is a bright yellow to green, deeply grooved, oval fruit the size of an orange. Sliced horizontally, the fruit looks like a five sided 'star'. They should be juicy and crisp in texture with a refreshing taste somewhat similar to a plum.

SANGRIA SPLASH RING

Prep time: 30 minutes   Chill time: 4 hours or overnight

2 pkg	(85 g **each**) JELL-O Lemon Jelly Powder	2 pkg
1½ cups	boiling dry white wine	375 mL
2 cups	chilled club soda	500 mL
1 Tbsp	orange liqueur (optional)	15 mL
3 cups	fruit: sliced strawberries, sliced star fruit, green and red grapes	750 mL

Additional fruit for garnish

▼ **DISSOLVE** jelly powders in boiling wine in medium bowl. Let cool to room temperature.

▼ **STIR** in club soda and liqueur. Chill until jelly is slightly thickened.

▼ **FOLD** in 3 cups (750 mL) fruit. Pour into 6 cup (1.5 L) mould or loaf pan. Chill 4 hours or overnight.

▼ **TO UNMOULD,** dip mould in warm water for about 10 seconds. Gently pull jelly from around edges with moist fingers. Place moistened serving plate on top of mould. Invert mould and plate; holding mould and plate together, shake slightly to loosen. Gently remove mould and centre jelly on plate. Garnish with additional fruit.

MAKES 12 servings.

TIP: Grease mould slightly with vegetable oil for easier removal.

▼ ▼ ▼ ▼ ▼ ▼

BUMBLEBERRY PIE

Prep time: 30 minutes   Chill time: 3 hours

1 pkg	(85 g) JELL-O Strawberry Jelly Powder	**1 pkg**
²/₃ cup	boiling water	**150 mL**
2 cups	ice cubes	**500 mL**
1 tub	(1 L) thawed COOL WHIP Whipped Topping	**1 tub**
¹/₃ cup	**each** mashed strawberries, whole raspberries and blueberries	**75 mL**
1	prepared 9 inch (23 cm) graham wafer crumb crust	**1**

Aditional fruit for garnish, if desired

▼ **DISSOLVE** jelly powder in boiling water.

▼ **ADD** ice cubes and stir until jelly starts to thicken about 3 to 5 minutes. Remove any unmelted ice.

▼ **BLEND** topping into jelly. Fold in fruit.

▼ **CHILL** until mixture is slightly thickened, about 15 minutes. Spoon into crumb crust. Chill for 3 to 4 hours.

▼ **JUST** before serving, garnish with additional fruit, if desired.

MAKES 8 servings.

TIP: Pie may be frozen 1 week. Thaw in refrigerator.

Above: Bumbleberry Pie

▼ ▼ ▼

RASPBERRY GLAZED LEMON MOUSSE CAKE

Prep time: 30 minutes   Chill time: 4 hours

27	ice wafers	**27**
1 pkg	(250 g) PHILADELPHIA Cream Cheese, softened	**1 pkg**
	Juice and rind of 1 lemon	
2 pkg	(85 g **each**) JELL-O Lemon Jelly Powder	**2 pkg**
1¼ cups	boiling water	**300 mL**
2 cups	ice cubes	**500 mL**
1 tub	(1 L) thawed COOL WHIP Whipped Topping	**1 tub**
½ cup	fresh raspberries	**125 mL**
1 pkg	(85 g) JELL-O Raspberry Jelly Powder	**1 pkg**
1 cup	**each** boiling water and ice cubes	**250 mL**

▼ **GREASE** a 9 inch (23 cm) springform pan. Place wafers around inside rim. Set aside.

▼ **BEAT** cream cheese in large bowl of electric mixer. Add lemon juice and rind, beating on low speed until blended.

▼ **DISSOLVE** lemon jelly powder in boiling water. Add ice cubes; stirring until slightly thickened, about 3 to 5 minutes. Remove unmelted ice.

▼ **ADD** jelly slowly to cream cheese mixture while beating on low speed. Increase speed and beat just until well blended.

▼ **FOLD** in whipped topping. Pour into prepared pan. Arrange raspberries on top and chill.

▼ **DISSOLVE** raspberry jelly powder in boiling water; add ice cubes and stir until slightly thickened. Immediately spoon over cake. Chill 4 hours.

MAKES 10 to 12 servings.

TIP: *For a lighter dessert substitute light cream cheese, COOL WHIP Light Whipped Topping and JELL-O Light Jelly Powder for regular products.*

DID YOU KNOW ABOUT ICE CUBES:

Ice cubes come in many shapes and sizes. This will effect your jelly set when using the 30 Minute Set Method. All sizes will work but your jelly may be slightly softer or firmer depending upon the shape you use.

▼ ▼ ▼ ▼ ▼ ▼ ▼

PEAR TERRINE

Prep time: 15 minutes   Chill time: 4 hours or overnight

2 pkg	(85 g **each**) JELL-O Lemon Jelly Powder	2 pkg
2 cups	boiling water	500 mL
1½ cups	cold water	375 mL
1 Tbsp	lemon juice	15 mL
1 can	(14 oz/398 mL) pear halves, drained	1 can
1 pkg	(250 g) PHILADELPHIA Cream Cheese, softened	1 pkg
¼ tsp	ground ginger	1 mL

▼ **DISSOLVE** jelly powders in boiling water. Add cold water and lemon juice. Measure 2 cups (500 mL) into 9 x 5 inch (23 x 13 cm) loaf pan. Chill until set, but not firm (jelly should be sticky to the touch), about 2 hours. Leave remaining jelly at room temperature.

▼ **MEANWHILE** finely chop pears and set aside.

▼ **BEAT** cheese until creamy. Very slowly whisk in remaining jelly, whisking until smooth. Blend in ginger.

▼ **CHILL** until slightly thickened. Stir in pears. Spoon over jelly in pan. Chill until firm 4 hours or overnight.

▼ **UNMOULD** on crisp lettuce and slice.

MAKES 10 servings.

TIP: If remaining jelly *sets too firm, heat to soften.*

SUNSET SALAD

Prep time: 10 minutes   Chill time: 4 hours or overnight

2 pkg	(85 g **each**) JELL-O Orange Pineapple or Lemon Jelly Powder	2 pkg
½ tsp	salt	2 mL
1½ cups	boiling water	375 mL
1 can	(14 oz/398 mL) crushed pineapple with juice, undrained	1 can
1 Tbsp	lemon juice	15 mL
1 cup	grated carrots	250 mL

▼ **DISSOLVE** jelly powder and salt in boiling water. Add pineapple with juice and lemon juice. Chill until slightly thickened about 45 minutes.

▼ **FOLD** in carrots. Pour into an 8 inch (20 cm) square pan. Chill until firm about 4 hours.

▼ **TO SERVE,** cut in squares and place on salad greens.

MAKES 8 to 10 servings.

TIP: Can also be poured into individual jelly mould or greased muffin pan.

Opposite page: Raspberry Glazed Lemon Mousse Cake

▼ ▼ ▼

Above:Pear Terrine, Sunset Salad

▼▼▼▼▼▼▼

FROZEN BANANA BOMBE

Prep time: 15 minutes   Freezing time: 4 hours or overnight

1 square	BAKER'S Semi-Sweet Chocolate, melted	1 sq
2	ripe bananas, mashed	2
1¼ cups	cold milk	300 mL
¼ cup	amber rum	50 mL
1 pkg	(4-serving size) JELL-O Vanilla Instant Pudding	1 pkg
1 pkg	(250 g) PHILADELPHIA Cream Cheese, softened	1 pkg
2 cups	thawed COOL WHIP Whipped Topping	500 mL

▼ **LINE** a large glass bowl with plastic wrap. Drizzle inside with melted chocolate; freeze to set.

▼ **MASH** bananas; set aside.

▼ **PLACE** milk, rum, pudding mix and cream-cheese in large bowl. Beat with electric mixer on medium speed until smooth. Stir in bananas.

▼ **FOLD** in whipped topping; spoon into prepared bowl. Freeze until firm.

▼ **REMOVE** from freezer, unmould and remove plastic wrap. Let stand at room temperature 5 minutes before slicing to serve.

MAKES 8 servings.

TIP: Substitute orange juice for the rum, if desired. Leftover COOL WHIP Whipped Topping may be refrozen.

CHERRY ALMOND CHEESE SQUARES

Prep time: 20 minutes   Freezing time: 2 hours

40	graham wafers	40
2 pkg	(250 g **each**) PHILADELPHIA Cream Cheese, softened	2 pkg
3 cups	cold milk, divided	750 mL
2 pkg	(4-serving size **each**) JELL-O Vanilla Instant Pudding	2 pkg
1 tsp	almond extract	5 mL
1 tub	(500 mL) thawed COOL WHIP Whipped Topping	1 tub
1 can	(19 oz/540 mL) cherry pie filling	1 can

▼ **ARRANGE** half of the cookies on bottom of 13 x 9 inch (33 x 23 cm) pan, cutting to fit if necessary.

▼ **BEAT** cream cheese at low speed of electric mixer until smooth. Gradually beat in 1 cup (250 mL) of the milk. In another bowl, combine pudding mix, remaining 2 cups (500 mL) of the milk and almond extract; whisk until blended. Add to cream cheese mixture and blend well. Fold in whipped topping.

▼ **SPREAD** half of the pudding mixture over cookies.

Arrange second layer of cookies on top. Top with remaining pudding mixture.

▼ **FREEZE** 2 hours. Let stand at room temperature 20 minutes before cutting into squares.

▼ **SPOON** cherry pie filling over each square.

MAKES 16 servings.

TIP: Use chocolate pudding, if desired.

▼▼▼

Above: *Cherry Almond Cheese Squares,*
Frozen Banana Bombe

JIGG-O-LANTERN

Prep time: 15 minutes   Chill time: 30 minutes

1 pkg	(85 g) JELL-O Juicy Orange Jelly Powder	1 pkg
1 cup	boiling water	250 mL
2 cups	vanilla ice cream, softened	500 mL

Assorted candies

▼ **DISSOLVE** jelly powder in boiling water. Cool to room temperature.

▼ **ADD** ice cream by spoonfuls, whisking until smooth.

▼ **POUR** into dessert dishes. Chill until set, about 30 minutes.

▼ **MAKE** "pumpkin" faces on jelly with candies.
Makes 4 servings.

TIP: Decorate with candies no more than 1 hour before serving or candies may "weep".

WORM CAKES

Prep time: 30 minutes   Chill time: 3 hours

24	white cupcakes	24
1 pkg	(85 g) JELL-O Berry Black Jelly Powder	1 pkg
1 cup	boiling water	250 mL
2 cups	thawed COOL WHIP Whipped Topping	500 mL

Gummy worms, chocolate wafer crumbs

▼ **PLACE** cupcakes in muffin tins. Pierce cupcakes with a large fork at ¼ inch (.5 cm) intervals; about 3 to 5 times.

▼ **DISSOLVE** jelly powder in boiling water. Using a teaspoon carefully pour the jelly over each cupcake.

▼ **REFRIGERATE** 3 hours. Dip muffin pan in warm water 10 seconds; unmould onto serving plate.

Frost with whipped topping.

▼ **GARNISH** with gummy worms and wafer crumbs to resemble 'dirt'. Store frosted cupcakes in refrigerator.

MAKES 24 servings.

TIP: These can be made in advance and frozen for 1 week.

Next page: Jigg-O-Lantern

▼ ▼ ▼

SWAMP WATER

Prep time: 5 minutes

2 cups	cold milk	**500 mL**
1 pkg	(85 g) JELL-O Berry Black Jelly Powder	**1 pkg**
2½ cups	vanilla ice cream or frozen yogurt	**625 mL**

▼ **POUR** milk in blender. Add jelly powder and ice cream; cover.

▼ **BLEND** at high speed 30 seconds or until smooth.

▼ **POUR** into glasses. Serve immediately.

Makes about 4 cups (1 L).

Variation:

▼ **ADD** JELL-O Juicy Orange Jelly Powder instead to make a "fizzy acid" beverage.

TIP: Freeze glasses for ½ hour before filling for "frosty" look.

Above: Worm Cakes, Swamp Water

Above: Tombstone Squares

▼ ▼ ▼ ▼ ▼ ▼

TOMBSTONE SQUARES

Prep time: 30 minutes   Chill time: 2 hours or overnight

2½ cups	chocolate wafer crumbs, divided	625 mL
⅓ cup	melted butter	75 mL
2 pkg	(85 g **each**) JELL-O Juicy Orange Jelly Powder	2 pkg
1½ cups	boiling water	375 mL
¾ cup	orange juice	175 mL
	Ice cubes	
1 tub	(1 L) thawed COOL WHIP Whipped Topping	1 tub

Decorations: Assorted rectangular-shaped cookies, writing gels, coloured coconut and candy

▼ **MIX** 2 cups (500 mL) of the wafer crumbs and melted butter; press firmly into bottom of a 13 x 9 inch (33 x 23 cm) pan.

▼ **DISSOLVE** jelly powder in boiling water. Combine orange juice and ice cubes to make 1¾ cups (425 mL). Add to jelly, stirring until ice is almost melted. Remove unmelted ice. Pour over crust. Chill until slightly thickened, about 1¼ hours.

▼ **TOP** with whipped topping.

▼ **SPRINKLE** remaining ½ cup (125 mL) wafer crumbs over whipped topping. Decorate cookies with icings to make "tombstones" and stand on top of dessert with coconut and candies to resemble a graveyard. Cut into squares.

MAKES 15 to 18 servings.

TIP: Small tubes of coloured writing gels work well for writing on cookies and are available at most grocery stores.

DIXIE SPIDERS

Prep time: 15 minutes   Chill time: 2 hours

2 pkg	(85 g **each**) JELL-O Berry Black Jelly Powder	2 pkg
1¼ cups	boiling water	300 mL
6	(3 oz /85 mL) paper cups	6

Licorice allsorts or other decorating candies
String licorice cut into 3 inch (7.5 cm) pieces

▼ **DISSOLVE** jelly powder in boiling water, stirring until completely dissolved, about 2 minutes. Pour into paper cups.

▼ **REFRIGERATE** until firm, at least 2 hours.

▼ **CAREFULLY** peel away paper cups from jelly. Slice a thin layer from long side to help 'spider' sit flat. Insert 3 licorice pieces on each side of

spider for legs; place licorice allsorts on top for eyes.

MAKES 6 spiders.

TIP: For a fun kids party, let the children help in decorating their own 'spider'.

▼ ▼ ▼

WITCHES BREW

Prep time: 15 minutes   Chill time: 2 hours

Hand

2 pkg	(85 g **each**) JELL-O Berry Black Jelly Powder	2 pkg
1½ cups	boiling water	375 mL

Eye Balls

1 pkg	(85 g) JELL-O Juicy Orange Jelly Powder	1 pkg
¾ cup	boiling water	175 mL
¼ cup	whole blueberries	50 mL

Prepared Eerie Orange KOOL-AID

HAND

▼ **DISSOLVE** jelly powder in boiling water, stirring until completely dissolved, about 2 minutes.

▼ **POUR** into a greased 8 inch (20 cm) baking pan.

▼ **REFRIGERATE** until firm, about 2 hours.

▼ **TRACE** outline of a small hand on a piece of paper. Cut out the pattern and place on top of set jelly. Using a knife, cut around the pattern. Carefully pull the 'hand' away from the baking pan.

▼ **PLACE** 'hand' in punch bowl; allowing 'fingers' to hang over sides of bowl.

EYE BALLS

▼ **DISSOLVE** jelly powder in boiling water, stirring until completely dissolved, about 2 minutes.

▼ **POUR** into round or square ice cube trays. Refrigerate until partially set. Poke a blueberry into the centre of each jelly eye ball; place in refrigerator until completely set.

▼ **PLACE** 'eye balls' around inside of punch bowl.

▼ **POUR** in prepared orange drink mix.

MAKES 10 to 12 servings.

> *TIP: Use left over black jelly to make individual 'fingers' or cut into pieces and serve with fresh fruit.*

Above: Witches Brew

▼ ▼ ▼

CROWN JEWEL DESSERT

Prep time: 40 minutes   Chill time: 4 hours or overnight

1 pkg	(85 g **each**) JELL-O Strawberry and Lime Jelly Powders	**1 pkg**
1 pkg	(85 g) JELL-O Strawberry-Kiwi Jelly Powder	**1 pkg**
3 cups	boiling water	**750 mL**
1½ cups	cold water	**375 mL**
1 pkg	(125 g/4.4 oz) 'bakery style' lady fingers	**1 pkg**
1 tub	(500 mL) thawed COOL WHIP Whipped Topping	**1 tub**

▼ **PREPARE** strawberry and lime jelly powders separately, as directed on package, reducing **cold** water to ½ cup (125 mL) for **each**. Pour **each** into an 8 inch (20 cm) square pan. Chill until set, about 1 hour.

▼ **PREPARE** strawberry-kiwi jelly powder as directed on package reducing **cold** water to ½ cup (125 mL). Chill until slightly thickened.

▼ **TRIM** length of one end of each lady finger to fit pan. Line the sides of 9 inch (23 cm) springform pan with cut lady fingers. (See tip below).

▼ **FOLD** whipped topping into slightly thickened strawberry-kiwi jelly; gently fold in red and green jelly cut into ½ inch (1 cm) cubes.

▼ **CAREFULLY** spoon into pan. Chill until firm, about 4 hours or overnight.

MAKES 12 servings.

> ***TIPS:*** *DO NOT add fresh kiwi to jelly as it will not set. Use your favourite flavours of JELL-O to create your own flavour combination, if desired.*

DID YOU KNOW ABOUT LADY FINGERS:

Lady fingers come in many different types. Types may be interchanged in recipes.

1. Giant Lady Fingers

A soft cookie type found in the cookie section of the grocery store. They come in 150 g (5.3 oz) packages.

2. Bakery Style Lady Fingers

They are found mostly in the bakery section of the grocery store. They are soft in texture. Packages usually contain 24 fingers.

3. Sugar Coated Biscuits (Champagne biscuits)

They are found in the baking or cookie section of the grocery store. These are crisp in texture. They come in packages of 24, about 400 g.

3. Ice Wafers

They are found in the cookie section of the grocery store and come in vanilla, chocolate or strawberry. Packages are 200 g and contain 21 wafers.

Opposite page: Crown Jewel Dessert

Above: Celebration Rainbow Cake

▼ ▼ ▼ ▼ ▼ ▼

CELEBRATION RAINBOW CAKE

Prep time: 10 minutes   Baking time: 30 minutes   Chill time: 4 hours

1 pkg	(2-layer size) white cake mix	**1 pkg**
2 pkg	(85 g **each**) JELL-O Jelly Powder, any flavours	**2 pkg**
2 cups	boiling water	**500 mL**
1 tub	(1 L) thawed COOL WHIP Whipped Topping	**1 tub**
	Toasted flaked coconut (optional)	
	Gumdrops (optional)	

▼ **LINE** bottoms and grease sides of two 9 inch (23 cm) cake pans.

▼ **PREPARE** and bake cake mix as directed on package.

▼ **COOL** in pans 15 minutes; do not remove from pans.

▼ **DISSOLVE** each package of jelly powder separately in 1 cup (250 mL) boiling water.

▼ **POKE** cakes with fork at ½ inch (1 cm) intervals.

▼ **DRIZZLE** one flavour jelly over one cake. Repeat with second cake layer and jelly flavour. Chill 4 hours.

▼ **UNMOULD** one cake onto serving plate, cover with some of the whipped topping. Unmould second cake onto first. Frost top and sides with remaining whipped topping. Sprinkle with coconut and garnish with flattened gumdrops, if desired. Chill.

MAKES 10 servings.

TIP: Flatten gumdrops with a rolling pin. Cut into flower petal shape. Roll one to make a tight "bud". Add 2 or more "petals" around centre to make flower. Cut a green gum drop for "stem" and "leaves".

RAINBOW RIBBON

Prep time: 3 hours   Chill time: 4 hours or overnight

5 pkg	(85 g **each**) JELL-O Jelly Powder, any 5 different flavours	**5 pkg**
6¼ cups	boiling water	**1.55 L**
1 cup	sour cream, plain yogurt, or vanilla ice cream	**250 mL**

▼ **DISSOLVE** 1 pkg jelly powder in 1¼ cups (300 mL) of the boiling water.

▼ **POUR** ¾ cup (175 mL) of the jelly into 8 cup (2 L) ring mould. Chill until set but not firm, about 15 minutes.

▼ **CHILL** remaining jelly in bowl until slightly thickened; gradually blend in 3 Tbsp (45 mL) of the sour cream. Spoon over jelly in mould. Chill until set but not firm, about 20 to 25 minutes.

▼ **REPEAT** with remaining jelly flavours.

▼ **CHILL** until firm, about 4 hours or overnight.

▼ **TO UNMOULD,** dip mould in warm water for about 10 seconds. Gently pull jelly from around edges with moist fingers. Place moistened serving plate on top of mould. Invert mould and plate; holding mould and plate together, shake slightly to loosen. Gently remove mould and centre jelly on plate.

MAKES 12 servings.

TIP: Use a wire whisk to add sour cream for a smoother jelly mixture.

▼ ▼ ▼

▼▼▼▼▼▼

Above: Rainbow Ribbon Dessert

▼▼▼

▼ ▼ ▼ ▼ ▼ ▼

PEACH MELBA DESSERT

Prep time: 1½ hours   Chill time: 4 hours or overnight

1 pkg	(85 g) JELL-O Raspberry Jelly Powder	1 pkg
2 cups	boiling water, divided	500 mL
1½ cups	vanilla ice cream, softened	375 mL
1 pkg	(85 g) JELL-O Peach or Lemon Jelly Powder	1 pkg
¾ cup	cold water	175 mL
1 can	(14 oz/398 mL) sliced peaches, drained	1 can
½ cup	fresh or frozen, thawed, raspberries	125 mL

▼ **DISSOLVE** raspberry jelly powder in 1 cup (250 mL) boiling water. Add ice cream by spoonfuls and whisk until melted and smooth. Pour into 6 cup (1.5 L) glass serving bowl. Chill until set but not firm, about 2 hours.

▼ **MEANWHILE** dissolve peach jelly powder in remaining 1 cup (250 mL) boiling water. Add cold water. Chill until slightly thickened, about 1¼ hours.

▼ **ARRANGE** peach slices and raspberries on ice cream layer in bowl. Gently spoon peach jelly over fruit. Chill until firm, about 4 hours or overnight.

MAKES 10 servings.

> **TIP:** *Peach jelly should be of egg white consistency before spooning over fruit - add slowly. This will ensure fruit does not float.*

Above: Peach Melba Dessert

Above: Strawberry Romanoff Dessert,
Melon Bubble

▼▼▼▼▼▼▼

MELON BUBBLE

Prep time: 10 minutes   Chill time: 30 minutes

1 pkg	(85 g) JELL-O Fruit Fiesta or Lemon Jelly Powder	1 pkg
1 cup	boiling water	250 mL
2 cups	ice cubes	500 mL
1 cup	melon balls	250 mL

▼ **PREPARE** jelly powder according to 30 Minute Set Method on package. Set aside ⅔ cup (150 mL) of slightly thickened jelly.

▼ **STIR** melon balls into remaining jelly; spoon into dessert dishes.

▼ **BEAT** reserved jelly with electric mixer until fluffy and doubled in volume. Spoon over first fruited layer.

▼ **CHILL** until set, 30 minutes.

MAKES 4 servings.

TIP: For best results when beating jelly, place in a 4 cup (1 L) pyrex measuring cup and beat on high speed.

STRAWBERRY ROMANOFF DESSERT

Prep time: 30 minutes   Chill time: 4 hours or overnight

2 pkg	(85 g **each**) JELL-O Strawberry Jelly Powder	2 pkg
2 cups	boiling water	500 mL
3 Tbsp	orange liqueur or orange juice	45 mL
½ cup	cold water	125 mL
2 cups	thawed COOL WHIP Whipped Topping	500 mL
1 pkg	(300 g) frozen unsweetened strawberries, thawed (do not drain)	1 pkg

▼ **DISSOLVE** jelly powders in boiling water. Measure 1¼ cups (300 mL) jelly; add undrained strawberries. Into remaining jelly add liqueur and cold water. Chill until slightly thickened, about 1¼ hours.

▼ **FOLD** topping into chilled jelly. Pour into a 6 cup (1.5 L) glass serving bowl. Carefully spoon reserved jelly mixture over layer in bowl. Chill until firm, about 4 hours or overnight.

MAKES 8 servings.

TIP: For Raspberry Romanoff, substitute JELL-O Raspberry Jelly Powder and frozen whole raspberries. Recipe may be doubled.

▼▼▼

*Above: Lemon Charlotte With
Raspberry Sauce*

▼ ▼ ▼ ▼ ▼ ▼

LEMON CHARLOTTE WITH RASPBERRY SAUCE

Prep time: 40 minutes   Chill time: 4 hours or overnight

Lemon Charlotte

1½ pkg	(3 oz/85 g **each**) lady fingers*	1½ pkg
1 pkg	(113 g) JELL-O Lemon Pie Filling	1 pkg
1 pkg	(250 g) PHILADELPHIA Cream Cheese, softened	1 pkg
1 envelope	(7 g) unflavoured gelatin	1 envelope
2 Tbsp	lemon juice	25 mL
1 tsp	grated lemon rind	5 mL
1 tub	(500 mL) thawed COOL WHIP Whipped Topping	1 tub

Or use 2 pkg (200 g each) Raspberry Swiss Rolls, sliced

Raspberry Sauce

1 pkg	(300 g) frozen unsweetened raspberries, thawed	1 pkg
⅓ cup	granulated sugar	75 mL

LEMON CHARLOTTE:

▼ **ARRANGE** lady fingers on sides and bottom of 9 inch (23 cm) springform pan. (Refer to page 115 for tips on lady fingers.) (If desired, brush lady fingers with Sherry before placing in pan.)

▼ **PREPARE** lemon pie filling mix as directed on package, reserving the egg whites. Beat cream cheese until light and fluffy. Add warm pie filling; mix well.

▼ **SPRINKLE** gelatin over lemon juice; let stand 5 minutes. Stir into hot pie filling with lemon rind. Cover surface of mixture with plastic wrap; chill to cool down but not set, about 30 minutes.

▼ **BEAT** egg whites until stiff peaks form; fold into topping. Gently whisk lemon mixture until smooth. Fold into topping mixture. Spoon mixture into prepared pan.

▼ **CHILL** at least 4 hours or overnight. If desired garnish with slivers of candied lemon peel. Serve with raspberry sauce.

MAKES 10 to 12 servings.

RASPBERRY SAUCE:

▼ **COMBINE** raspberries and sugar. Heat over medium heat until boiling. Remove. Sieve to remove seeds, if desired. Chill.

TIP: To make Candied Peel - Remove peel from one lemon. Cut into thin strips. Cover rind with cold water. Bring to a boil; drain water. Repeat process 3 times. Combine ½ cup (125 mL) water and ¼ cup (50 mL) sugar in saucepan. Bring to a boil. Add lemon strips. Simmer until strips are translucent. Remove from syrup and place on waxed paper. Decorate top of cake with peel.

▼ ▼ ▼

FRUIT FLAN DELUXE

Prep time: 30 minutes   Baking time: 12 minutes   Chill time: 3 hours

1 cup	all-purpose flour	**250 mL**
2 Tbsp	icing sugar	**25 mL**
½ cup	butter	**125 mL**
1 pkg	(6-serving size) JELL-O Vanilla Pudding and Pie Filling	**1 pkg**
2½ cups	milk	**625 mL**
	Any selection of canned or fresh fruit (i.e. strawberries, peaches, apricots, pears, grapes, mandarin oranges, blueberries)	
½ cup	KRAFT Apricot Jam	**125 mL**
1 Tbsp	lemon juice	**15 mL**
1 Tbsp	orange liqueur or orange juice	**15 mL**

▼ **SIFT** flour and icing sugar together in mixing bowl. Cut in butter until mixture resembles coarse meal. Form into a ball. Chill 30 minutes. Press firmly onto bottom and sides of a 9 inch (23 cm) flan pan or pie plate. Bake at 425°F (220°C) for 10 to 12 minutes until golden brown. Cool in pan.

▼ **PREPARE** pudding with the milk as directed on package. Place plastic wrap on surface of pudding; chill 30 minutes.

▼ **WHISK** chilled pudding until smooth. Pour into flan shell.

▼ **ARRANGE** fruits attractively to cover surface of pudding.

▼ **HEAT** apricot jam, lemon juice and liqueur over low heat until melted. Remove from heat and sieve. Cool slightly and spoon over fruit.

▼ **CHILL** until set, 3 hours. Remove from flan pan and serve.

MAKES 8 servings.

TIP: For easy mixing, the pastry may be made in a food processor.

Above: Fruit Flan Deluxe

LIGHT'N FRUITY RASPBERRY PIE

Prep time: 20 minutes   Chill time: 3 hours

1 pkg	(85 g) JELL-O Raspberry Jelly Powder	**1 pkg**
²⁄₃ cup	boiling water	**150 mL**
2 cups	ice cubes	**500 mL**
1 tub	(1 L) thawed COOL WHIP Whipped Topping	**1 tub**
1 cup	raspberries, fresh or frozen, thawed and drained	**250 mL**
1	prepared 9 inch (23 cm) graham wafer crumb crust	**1**

▼ **DISSOLVE** jelly powder in boiling water. Add ice cubes and stir constantly until jelly starts to thicken, 3 to 5 minutes. Remove any unmelted ice.

▼ **WHISK** in whipped topping gently until smooth. Fold in fruit. Chill until slightly thickened, about 15 minutes.

▼ **SPOON** into crust. Chill 3 hours.

MAKES 8 servings.

TIP: A wire whisk works well to blend jelly and whipped topping.

Above: Light'n Fruity Raspberry Pie

▼ ▼ ▼

▼ ▼ ▼ ▼ ▼ ▼ ▼

LAYERED PINEAPPLE SALAD

Prep time: 15 minutes   Chilling time: 4 hours or overnight

1 pkg	(85 g) JELL-O Lemon Jelly Powder	**1 pkg**
4 cups	boiling water, divided	**1 L**
1 cup	miniature marshmallows	**250 mL**
1 pkg	(250 g) PHILADELPHIA Cream Cheese, softened	**1 pkg**
2 cups	thawed COOL WHIP Whipped Topping	**500 mL**
1 can	(14 oz/398 mL) crushed pineapple, drained	**1 can**
½ cup	chopped walnuts	**125 mL**
2 pkg	(85 g **each**) JELL-O Strawberry Jelly Powder	**2 pkg**

▼ **DISSOLVE** lemon jelly powder in 1 cup (250 mL) boiling water; cool slightly. Add marshmallows and cream cheese. Beat with an electric mixer on low speed until smooth; chill until slightly thickened.

▼ **STIR** whipped topping, pineapple and walnuts into partially set jelly. Pour into a 2 qt (2 L) deep bowl. Chill until set but not firm, about 1 hour.

▼ **DISSOLVE** strawberry jelly powder in remaining 3 cups (750 mL) boiling water; cool.

▼ **POUR** cooled jelly over lemon cream cheese mixture and chill until set, about 4 hours or overnight.

MAKES 10 to 12 servings.

TIP: A great party recipe. Eliminate walnuts, if desired.

Above: Layered Pineapple Salad

▼ ▼ ▼

INDEX

▼ ▼ ▼ ▼ ▼ ▼

▼ ▼ ▼